Vancouver Rainy Day Guide

Vancouver
Rainy Day Guide

by
Paula Brook

Illustrations by
Marion Dahl

Chinook Editions

**Published by Chronicle Books
in association with Solstice Press**

Produced by Mary Schierman, Karen Cathcart, Connie Bollinger, Ken Yuhasz, and Danny Breece under the direction of Ivar Nelson and Patricia Hart at North Country Book Express in Moscow, Idaho.

Cover photograph: Rick Semple.

ISBN: 0-87701-315 2

Chronicle Books
870 Market Street
San Francisco, CA 94102

Distributed in Canada by:
Raincoast Book Distribution Ltd.
15 West 6th Avenue
Vancouver, B.C. V5Y 1K2

Printed in the United States of America

Table of Contents

INTRODUCTION

"The weatherman says: chances for an Indian summer are nil. Chances for an Indian fall are slim. Chances for a long wet winter are good. Showers today, rain tomorrow."

I was hunched over a rain-splashed picnic table in our neighbourhood park, reading *The Province* one typically grey Vancouver fall morning, when that weather report caught my eye. I recall making a mental note (I was gumboot-deep in research for this book at the time) about how that little forecast precisely captured the Vancouver attitude toward rain. People here adopt a tone of "can you believe it?" jocularity in the face of day-in, day-out drizzle, turning up their collars against the damp and carrying on. It seems no amount of rain (not even the average 55 inches that falls 156 days out of each 365) can turn our hearts against this remarkable city.

You can do almost everything on a rainy day that you can do on a sunny one, but you must approach it with a rainy-day attitude. You can hike through the woods, but you had better dress appropriately and stick to bark mulch trails. You can go window-shopping, but do yourself a favour and head for one of the ethnic neighbourhoods where you're never more than a dash away from a Chinese teahouse or a steamy espresso bar. If you have kids in tow, why not take advantage of the rain to do something you'd never consider when the sun is out—like tunnel underground, way underground, at the Britannia Mining Museum?

Rain brings out creative resources. In a wet city like Vancouver, sunshine comes as a treat and people greet it by dropping the activity at hand and making for the nearest beach or park. You don't have to do anything to enjoy sunshine. But when the clouds roll in, it's back to the drawing boards: Now what are we going to do?

This book attempts to answer that question, both for the benefit of residents and visitors. I have tried to include enough offbeat suggestions to give natives pause to wonder whether we're even talking about the same Vancouver. And I hope to answer the call of tourists who wake up each morning of their limited stays to forecasts like the one printed above. There is no reason under the clouds why their visit to Vancouver should be any less enjoyable just because the sun decided to take a vacation at the same time.

One cautionary note: you can be sure that by the time you read this at least one of the restaurants listed has gone out of business, an art gallery has moved into new premises, somebody has put a "No Pedestrians" sign on one of my favourite walks, and (I guarantee this) prices have gone up across the board. You are well advised to call ahead wherever appropriate.

The World's Fair is coming! Centered on the north shore of False Creek, Expo 86 will run for five months starting in the the spring of 1986. Preparations for the Fair are changing the face of Vancouver, adding an excitement to the town which no amount of sun can burn away.

It would be impossible to list all the people—friends, relatives, the guy sitting at the next booth in the Montgomery Cafe—who shared their favourite wet-weather pastimes and haunts with me. The Vancouver Public Library, the Downtown Vancouver Association, Park Board, Tourism B.C., Greater Vancouver Visitors Bureau and City Archives placed a wealth of information at my fingertips.

Mac Parry, Don Stanley, Judie Hogan and all my other work mates at *Vancouver Magazine* gave me the time and space I needed to put this book together, not to mention a lot of invaluable suggestions. Thanks also to Don McLellan for sharing his nightlife insights with me, to Anne Petrie for sharing her Secrets, and to Mark Schneider for introducing me to my publisher and editor, Ivar Nelson.

This book is dedicated to my husband Shaw Saltzberg, who has never taken more walks, visited more landmarks or drunk more cappuccino in his entire life, and to my daughter Abby whose socks are still drying on the radiator.

Paula Brook
Vancouver, Spring 1984

GET AROUND

Ready, Set

If you are a non-Canadian visiting Vancouver, your first concern will be getting a good exchange for your currency. That's not easy, should you be carrying Moroccan dirham or Gibraltar pounds. Major exchange brokers (**Deak-Perera** is the largest, 687-6111) handle dozens of currencies that the banks don't, and at good rates. They are generally competitive in the common currencies as well, though on the day I called, their exchange on the U.S. dollar was a shade lower than that of the banks. A rule of thumb: banks are best, private brokers are usually a better deal than the airport exchange counter (three cents difference the day I surveyed) and the airport is slightly better than most hotels.

Take a Map

Threatening clouds compel a certain amount of forethought. You don't want to get stuck at the rain-slicked, wind-swept corner of Burrard and Robson looking for a place to buy a map, wishing you had worn a hooded poncho. Play it safe. Rain or shine, head for the **Greater Vancouver Convention and Visitors Bureau** in the Royal Centre Mall, under the Hyatt Regency Hotel at Burrard and Georgia. (Mon.-Sat. 9:30 a.m. to 5 p.m. in winter, 8:30 a.m. to 7 p.m. in summer, 682-2222.) The bureau publishes an accommodation guide as well as the very handy quarterly magazine, *Greater Vancouver Visitors Guide*, offering tour suggestions, a map of attractions and shopping guide. They also publish a few "things to do" sheets including a not very exciting *Things To Do On Rainy Days* list (but then, I'm biased) and a run-down of *Educational and Industrial Tours*. You can also pick up the bureau's *Self-Guided Walking Tour of Downtown* and head off in search of malls and monuments.

The most current and complete local calendar of events is in the "What's On" section of the downtown weekly newspaper *The Westender*, available in street boxes and shops all over the downtown (also at the bureau's Royal Centre stand). Judith Hogan's "In Town" column in the calendar section of the monthly *Vancouver Magazine* is an excellent guide which leans toward visual and performing arts.

As for the two local dailies, the weekend editions have the best ads and listings. The *Vancouver Sun*'s Friday

VANCOUVER

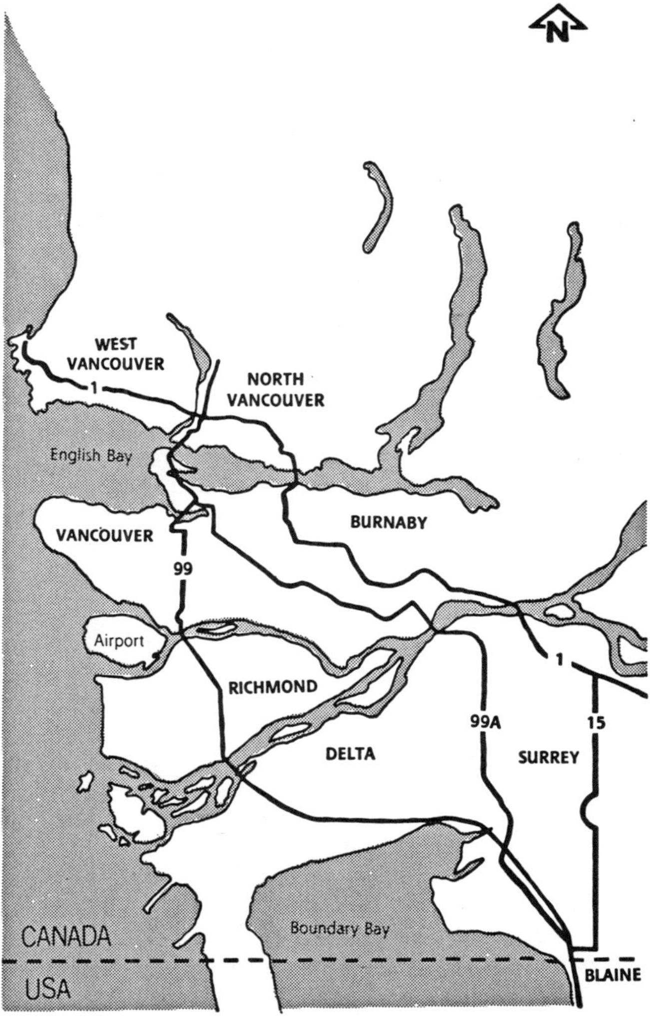
N
WEST VANCOUVER
1
NORTH VANCOUVER
English Bay
VANCOUVER
BURNABY
99
Airport
RICHMOND
1
99A
15
DELTA
SURREY
CANADA
Boundary Bay
USA
BLAINE

"What's On" section gives you a good browse through current events and entertainment, and *The Sunday Province* serves it up in neat tabloid form. It's easy to miss, but the best movie and performance calendar we get out of our dailies is the "Entertainment" section front of *The Sun* on the first day of the month. If it's rock music you're looking for, *The Georgia Straight* is your paper, available at most newsstands and in downtown street boxes. Their "Time Out" section has all the important club and concert gigs, surrounded by backstage interviews and record reviews.

If your focus of interest goes beyond Vancouver to British Columbia, make an information stop at **Tourism B.C.** in Robson Square, 800 Robson (Mon.-Fri. 8:30 a.m. to 5 p.m., Sat. 10 to 6 in winter, daily 8:30 to 6 in summer, 668-2300). They have brochures on the key city and province attractions, transit information, park guides and assorted maps. The *Map of Greater Vancouver, Fraser Valley & Victoria* is sold here and at bookstores and kiosks all over town for $1.50. It is the most comprehensive street map you could want—possibly more comprehensive (and bulky) than you can comfortably use. I like the compact *Visitors Map* published by Tourism B.C. and available free at either of the information bureaus.

Coat Yourself

This is Vancouver, not Rangoon. You don't need to cover yourself head to toe in rubberized canvas to stay dry. In fact, few people I know even bother to carry umbrellas when the sky is threatening rain because nine times out of ten it is going to just keep threatening all day long, with the odd interval of drizzle. If you are just dashing from place to place, you can brave it in a cloth coat with a newspaper over your head.

But if it is really raining, and the forecast says more of the same, dress for it. Gore-Tex is the best thing you can wear if you are planning to be outside for extended periods. Typically, Gore-Tex jackets sell for $100, pants for $50 to $80 at outdoorsy shops like **Mountain Equipment Co-op** (428 West 8th, 872-7858), **Coast Mountain Sports** (1822 West 4th, 731-6181), **Taiga Works** (1675 West 2nd, 731-2311), the Canadian Hostelling Association's **Pack and Boots Shop** (3425 West Broadway, 738-3128) or **Great Outdoors Equipment** (201 Lonsdale, North Vancouver, 980-3313). You can seriously hike in these rain suits, or casually stroll. They are lightweight, have lots of convenient pockets and zippers, and fold down to a compact bundle to stuff into your carry-all when the sun comes out.

If you're a runner, don't even think twice about the weather. In Vancouver people jog through rain, sleet and gale-force winds, and the more intelligent ones even stay dry. You can buy light-weight Gore-Tex or coated nylon jogging suits at most sporting goods stores. **Sportif** (2674 West 4th, 736-6411) has the best selection, including Asics and Head brands for between $200 and $300 a suit. Pricey, indeed, but this miracle fabric never wears out.

More reasonably priced rubberized nylon jackets, ponchos and suits are available at many of these shops plus the department stores. Keep in mind that coated nylon doesn't breathe, so if you intend to tour strenuously be sure to get a garment with plenty of flaps and zippers for ventilation. Prices range from $130 for Peter Storm sailing suits at Mountain Co-op to $26 for a three-piecer (jacket, pants, hood) at **The Three Vets** (2200 Yukon St., 872-5475). If all you want is a purse-sized emergency coat that will stand you in good stead at the bus stop if not at The Four Season's Garden Lounge, pick up the $7 see-through special at Three Vets where they sell more rain coats on an average winter day than most shops have in stock.

I don't have to tell you where to buy an umbrella—they're everywhere. Just this one tip: The largest street umbrella you can buy is the Multi-Purpose model which sells for $25 at **B.C. Umbrella Manufacturing Co.** near Gastown (72 West Cordova, 683-2619). Two can walk comfortably under it.

The Large View

Using a map to get around the city can make you feel like an ostrich with your head in the sand. If you'd rather be an eagle, head for the cliffs and towers. Once you have studied the city below you, the map will make a lot more sense. Here are three of my favourite perches.

Harbour Centre Observation Deck (689-0421): The spaceship atop the mall and tower at 555 West Hastings is reached by an appetite-depressing ride in the Skylift Elevator on the outside of the tower—one good reason you should not have a heavy meal while you're up at the Ports of View Restaurant. (Remember, you've got to ride back down.) Information plaques and telescopes circling the deck help you identify the city's landmarks and, if it's not too overcast, the mountains and inlets beyond. There is an admission fee of $1.50 for adults, $1 for children under 12 (under six free) to get up to the deck. For

another $1.75 you can watch the excellent *Vancouver Discovery* sight-and-sound slide show, running for 25 minutes every hour on the hour. It's a sure bet for those who want to leave their hearts in Vancouver, and their stomachs at the top of Harbour Centre. To get there by bus, take #50, #3, #6 or #12 north on Granville St.

Queen Elizabeth Park (874-8336): This exquisitely landscaped park sits on the peak of Little Mountain—the highest elevation in the city core and very close to the geographic centre. You can drive up on a curving road, enjoying the views as you go, or take the #15 Cambie bus south along the west side of Burrard to 33rd, cross to the lowest parking lot and take the pedestrian path up. (It really is a little mountain.)

British Properties/Cypress Viewpoint: My choice, when I'm playing host to visiting friends or relatives, is to take a 20-minute drive up Hollyburn Mountain in West Vancouver, just as far as the first viewpoint parking lot where (if the clouds are not too low) there is a breathtaking vantage of the tangle of peninsulas, inlets, rivers and deltas that make up Greater Vancouver. On a sunny or very high-overcast day you can see the ring of mountains that frame it, from the peaks of Howe Sound and Vancouver Island to the Olympic Peninsula, Mount Baker and Burnaby Mountain. You get there by taking the Upper Levels (Trans Canada) Highway west toward Horseshoe Bay, taking the Cypress Bowl Rd. turnoff right up the mountain to the viewpoint.

If you're without a car, you can stick to the beautiful residential slopes of Hollyburn—the renowned British Properties where the only thing more spectacular than the homes is the view. There is a British Properties bus that takes a complete tour of the heights. You can transfer onto it from any of the buses that take you from the West Vancouver Transit stop downtown at Granville and Georgia to the Park Royal Shopping Centre.

Cruising: Land, Sea & Air

So your idea of walking is from doorstep to curb? You're looking for a way to get around on someone else's steam? Look no further. Vancouver offers scores of touring alternatives to trekking the slippery streets—and I'm not just talking about bus tours and harbour cruises. Why not go all out and hire a chauffeured 1947 vintage Rolls Royce? Or take a helicopter tour of downtown and Burrard Inlet for a real bird's eye view of the sights?

On Land

You can't go wrong with the ol' standby bus tour, especially if you choose one of the established lines. The **Gray Line** (872-8311) offers three and four-hour guided tours of the important sights, including a North Shore route that takes you over the Lions Gate Bridge to Capilano Canyon and a lovely evening shoreline tour up Howe Sound. Gray Line also operates the red double-deckers you've seen around town, taking visitors to Stanley Park, Gastown, Chinatown and the future site of Expo 86. Prices range from $12.50 to $19.50 (adults), about half that for children.

Maverick Coach Lines (255-1171) offers tours of greater distance, including a full-day excursion up the Sunshine Coast to Powell River and back (through the colourful "Beachcombers" TV town of Gibsons) for $33. Shorter tours include a drive up to the Whistler ski resort ($16.50) and to Minter Gardens in the Fraser Valley ($12).

Maverick also has three attractive city tour packages. You can tour the downtown plus Queen Elizabeth Park for three and a half hours, morning or afternoon, or do a similar length loop along the North Shore to Grouse Mountain, the British Properties, Cleveland Dam and Horseshoe Bay. Or combine them for a six and a half hour grand tour. Prices range from $14 to $29 for adults, $8 to $18 for children.

Town Tours (733-4711) offers more intimate mini-bus sightseeing, with one standard (but well designed) tour of Stanley Park, Granville Island, Queen Elizabeth Park, Chinatown, Gastown, Shaughnessy homes, Kits Beach and Robson St. It takes three and a half hours, leaves twice daily and costs $19 adults/$11 children.

An option most people don't think of is limousine rental. No, it's not just for stars. And no, it's not so very expensive. The typical rate is $35 to $40 an hour for a stretch Lincoln or Cadillac or a classic Rolls. Because you can fit up to six passengers in most of these limos, you get to tour in the lap of luxury with a personal chauffeur/guide, bar service, even a mini-TV, for as little as $6 per hour.

I once had the privilege of cruising the nightclubs in a real plum of an old Rolls from **Star Limousine** (874-0513). Star boss Randy Snider has eight of these reconditioned beauties, all right-hand drive, for his circuit of tours, including short city sightseeing drives and a nightclub tour which drops you at four local hot spots and guarantees you won't have to wait in line at the door. Alternately, you can design your own tour for $35 an hour.

Whatever your inclination, there is probably a chauffeured limo out there somewhere especially suited to you. Silver-haired ladies seem to look just right in the '58 Silver Cloud Rolls from **W.K. Limousine** ($35 an hour, two-hour minimum, 984-9668). The pinstriped crowd usually sticks with Cadillac factory limos from **B.C. Limousine** ($40 an hour, no minimum, 438-3571). And I'm not going to venture a guess who hires the white stretch Lincoln from **Lady Lincoln Limo** (738-3644) with its plush burgundy interior, colour TV and video, champagne bar, moonroof/sunroof and (of course) lady chauffeur—all for $40 for the first hour, $35 after that, or $150 for five hours.

By Sea

A good, thick mist gives a harbour cruise just the right atmosphere. There are a number of small charter companies that will take you around Vancouver's waterways, but the most reliable is **Harbour Ferries** (687-9558). It offers a 90-minute cruise on the old paddlewheeler *Constitution* from the marina at Coal Harbour (foot of Denman St.) around Burrard Inlet between the Lions Gate and Second Narrows Bridges, lively commentary included, for $10 (adults), $7.50 (seniors and students) and $5 (children). Its slightly more expensive Granville Island tour circles Stanley Park and enters English Bay to False Creek, berthing at noon for a lunch-and-tour stop on the island. Both cruises run Wednesday through Sunday all summer, Wednesdays and Sundays from Labour Day on.

If you are more interested in a brief water crossing than a tour, catch the **Sea-Bus** (324-3211) operated by the Greater Vancouver Transit System. It's a 12-minute ride from the old CPR Station at the north foot of Granville St. (downtown) to Lonsdale Quay in North Vancouver aboard an ultra-modern, 400-passenger ferry that slices through the still water like a fat knife through soft butter. It's a fun and inexpensive diversion, especially if you've got kids. You can get on the Sea-Bus with a valid transfer from connecting buses, or buy a ticket at either terminal. Have exact change ready: Adults 75¢, secondary students 35¢, children and seniors 30¢. Sailings are every 15 minutes Monday to Friday, every half-hour weekends, evenings and holidays. To avoid the crush of commuters, aim for sailing between 10 a.m. and 3 p.m. These ferries are wheelchair accessible, but pre-arrangements must be made.

A mere dinghy by comparison, the **False Creek Ferry** (734-2082) is nevertheless a picturesque and convenient way to travel from downtown to Granville Island, one of Vancouver's most popular strolling, shopping and browsing destinations for residents and tourists alike. The 12-passenger boat leaves every five minutes daily from the Aquatic Centre at the downtown foot of Burrard Bridge to the Granville Island Public Market. For just 75¢ you neatly avoid the island's one downfall—parking.

If you want to tour the Vancouver waters your own way, **Barbary Coast Yacht Basin** (669-0088) can provide you with virtually any kind of boat, from 24 to 120 footers, bareboat or skippered, power or sail. No need for concern if the water is a bit choppy—Vancouver's harbours are sufficiently protected to afford comfortable sailing in a 30-foot or larger craft any day of the year. Go down to the Coal Harbour marina and talk to Scott Hoffman or Irwin Kreiger about your needs. They can set you up with a stocked bar, picnic lunch and skipper-guide for an Indian Arm cruise that gives an unparalleled view of our coast city. "It's really special to see the city from the water, even in the rain," says assistant Brenda. She recommends Indian Arm on rough days, English Bay when it's calm. Prices range from $25 an hour if you want to skipper your own 24-foot, four-passenger "Sea Ranger" (8 hours for $170) to $295 for the 120-foot "Kona Winds" which accommodates a party of 100 including bar, chef and skipper. Bareboats (no skipper) are available only on a weekly basis.

Land & Sea

B.C. Rail's **Royal Hudson/Britannia** tour (info at the North Vancouver terminal, 987-5211) is probably the best package deal that the B.C. tourism industry has. I've done it twice, and look forward to the third time. First understand that I'm a prairie girl by birth, and in my first 20 years the most exciting transportation I encountered was riding in the cab of an International Harvester. Contrast that with hugging the sheer cliffs of Howe Sound aboard the historic "Royal Hudson" steam train en route from North Vancouver to Squamish, and back down the sound between glacial peaks on Harbour Ferries' excursion yacht "MV Britannia."

This is a summer tour only, Wednesdays and Sundays from Victoria Day in May to mid-September. You can take the boat and train in either direction, starting at 9:30 a.m. at the North Vancouver terminal if you're taking the train up, or at Harbour Ferries' marina on Coal Harbour to catch the Britannia. Either way, you get about two hours of the six-hour excursion to kick around the lumber port town of Squamish.

If you wake up with a craving for high tea at The Empress in Victoria, there is an easy way to get there via Pacific Coach Lines' **Sail by Coach** tour (683-9277). The Royal Victorian package costs $24 return, entails seven hours of transit on buses and B.C. Ferries, and leaves at least enough time to choke down a couple of crumpets and take a stroll down Government St. You choose your own bus time (buses leave both Victoria and Vancouver on even hours from 6 a.m. to 8 p.m. year-round) and just sit back and let the bus driver worry about catching the ferries between Tsawwassen and Swartz Bay. Even in the rain it's a lovely boat ride, weaving through gulf islands dense with forest, dotted with cliff-hanging cottages. The ferries are deluxe in every way but the cuisine. More accurately, the grub.

In the Air

If your stay in Vancouver is limited, and so is the visibility, you're not going to see much (if anything) of the mountains no matter what your vantage point. Best to get mountains right out of your head—pretend there aren't any and you won't be disappointed. (Then, when the cloud cover lifts to reveal forest-green peaks, fantasy-powdered in winter, so close you'll think you can touch them, it will be like a miracle.) Anyway, there is much more to Vancouver than mountains, and you can see it all from a plane or helicopter no matter how cloudy it is.

Chief pilot Ken Gagnon of **Sierra Air Services** (270-9448) recommends its "Flightseeing" float-plane tours for rainy days, heading west over the Gulf Islands or up Howe Sound. As long as the cloud cover is medium to high, you can take the six-hour ($249) tour up the Sunshine Coast to Chatterbox Falls on Jervis Inlet, then back down with a lunch stop at Gibsons. Shorter tours, like the 110-minute loop over the city, east to Burnaby Mountain and back around the North Shore, cost $69.50. The only flights Ken wouldn't tackle in the rain are up Garibaldi Mountain to Whistler or through the Fraser Canyon.

Harbour Air (688-1277) offers shorter tours, including a popular 20-minute circle over the Vancouver harbour, Lions Gate Bridge, Point Atkinson at the head of Howe Sound, back around to Point Grey (U.B.C.) and Granville Island. The tour in a three-passenger Cessna 185 is $80 for the group, $84 in the six-seater Beaver.

Helicopter touring is more expensive (typically $60 per person for 30 minutes) but also more fulfilling—especially for scenic photographers. Pilot Randy Wiens of **Nova Helicopters** (273-9732) can fly you from the airport in a wide circle around the city, or from Gastown for a more concentrated tour of downtown. **Wright Brothers Aviation** (525-4949) offers 15-minute tours from the Gastown helipad over landmarks such as Stanley Park, English Bay and the B.C. Place stadium on False Creek.

Accessible To The Handicapped

The best all-purpose guide book for the wheelchair-bound is called *Access Vancouver*, available from the **Canadian Paraplegic Association** (324-3611) or at the **Tourism B.C.** office in Robson Square (668-2300), sunken-gardens level. Incidentally, Robson Square is one of the city's most comprehensively accessible facilities for the handicapped, and houses a small theatre and gallery, restaurants, the architecturally striking new law courts and, in what used to be the old law courts, the exquisite new Vancouver Art Gallery. Here is an entire day of wheelchair-accessible touring.

Access Vancouver was researched by paraplegics employed by the Opportunity Rehabilitation Workshop, and while it is not an exhaustive listing of Vancouver's buildings and resources it certainly is accurate in what it does list. There are banks, churches, hospitals, hotels, restaurants, bars, shopping malls and a handful of recreation facilities. Most surprising is the relatively small number of places that are truly accessible. In the section on pubs, discos and nightclubs, for example, only three of 37 listings have entranceways, table arrangements and washrooms that require a minimum of elbow grease.

The booklet's only drawback is that by the time it was laboriously researched and published in 1982, it was slightly dated. (A revised edition is now in the works.) Still, there is more information for the handicapped here than in any any other single source, and you can't complain about the price (free).

An excellent listing of current tourist attractions, from museums to horseracing, comes out of Tourism B.C. annually in leaflet form, called simply *Attractions in Vancouver*. Each of 50-odd listings includes a note on wheelchair accessibility. Also free, at Robson Square.

Special Transit

Despite long and hard lobbying by service organizations and coalitions of the disabled, **B.C. Transit** (685-5131) is still far from making any commitment on customizing the regular city buses. Normally Vancouverites stand up staunchly for their home town in the age-old rivalry with Seattle—but not on this issue. Seattle has equipped 90 percent of its Metro buses with mechanical lifts at the door for those in wheelchairs or for those who are otherwise unable to manage the steps. Vancouver has put into action a special 83-vehicle fleet of customized mini-buses rather than make such a sweeping change, and while this independent system does its share of good work, it simply can't keep up with demand.

You are eligible for custom bus service if you have a disability that prevents you from using conventional buses. For between $1 and $1.50 (depending on distance within Greater Vancouver) these mini-buses will take wheelchair users to and from work, old or infirm people to medical appointments, and young or older disabled people to school. Recreation and entertainment are a second priority: if there is a bus not previously booked for one of the purposes above, you can use it to go shopping or to a movie. The rules apply to both residents and visitors. Try to reserve at least two to three days in advance, and if you have a recreational destination in mind your best chances will be between 10 a.m. and noon, or 1 p.m. to 3 p.m.

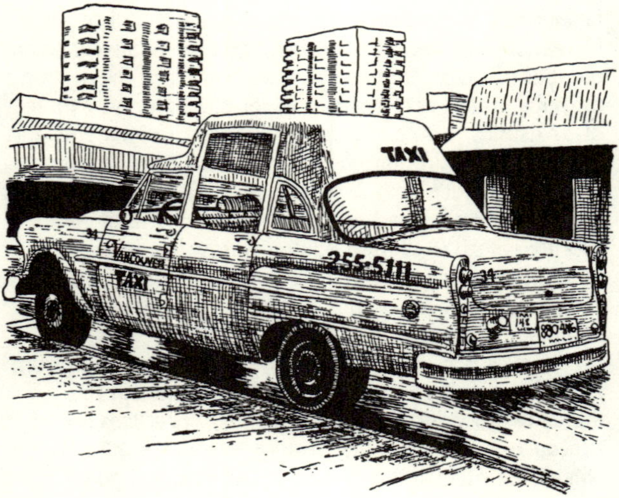

If you can afford taxi fare, your transit problems are over. **Vancouver Taxi** (255-5111) has a fleet of 30 customized Checker Cabs available on demand, for the same fare as conventional taxies: $1.40 flag, $1.20 a mile. They are absurd-looking vehicles, but wonderfully convenient, having a section cut out of the back seat and the roof raised to accommodate the wheelchair along with up to four other passengers. During rush hour, call at least half an hour ahead.

Parks and Recreation

The Park Board's philosophy is to integrate disabled people into regular recreational programs and activities as much as possible, rather than streaming them into separate facilities. To this end, they work with city planners on making facilities accessible, and in recent years there have been significant gains. The new **Riley Recreation Complex** (879-6222), two blocks west of 30th and Main, offers a community centre, ice arena, pool and health centre all on one level. Special needs groups, including wheelchair users, the blind, amputees and those with cerebral palsy, are regularly scheduled to use the facilities. **Douglas Park** (876-3371, 801 West 22nd) is another very accessible centre, offering a special

Wednesday afternoon program for handicapped teens (sports, crafts, outings and special events). There are all kinds of other such programs across the city. Plug into them through the **Park Board** (681-1141, local 31).

One of the most popular activities in this area is "adapted aquatics" (basically swimming and movement) which is offered at various times through the week at **Britannia** (253-4391) and **Percy Norman** (876-8804) pools. A new program called "Aqua Percept" at **Kensington Pool** (327-9401) uses water games to promote motor development. For details call 681-1141, local 18. Visitors are welcome to drop in for a trial session.

The board publishes a manual on exercise for wheelchair users, available free at all community centres. It also subsidize rates for disabled persons using any Vancouver parks and recreation facilities.

GET WET

Umbrella Tours

Of course it's entirely a personal choice whether to head out into the misty morning in your mackintosh, umbrella at the ready, or in your Gore-Tex jacket, hood up, jeans tucked into rubber boots.

I have broken up these touring ideas into sections depending on how wet you are likely to get. The Umbrella Tours do not require head-to-toe protection against the elements. They meander through core city areas, never taking you more than a few minutes' dash away from the shelter of an awning or (even better) a warm, dry cafe. These are suited to strollers of all ages, while the really wet tours in the next section (through marshes, around parks, deep into canyons) take a bit more toll on the old body.

Guided Walking Tours

If you happen to be in Vancouver in the early fall you may be lucky enough to catch the Downtown Vancouver Association's Historical Walkabout—a massive event which premiered in 1983 and promises to be a much talked-about walkabout for years to come. Rain or shine, thousands of Vancouverites and visitors pay the $6 registration and trek the seven km. route from Robson Square through Gastown to Yaletown and back, led by a small army of tour guides (including aldermen and journalists), everyone dressed in "Historical Team" T-shirts, toting maps of the city's finest old landmarks. The trek is usually held on a Sunday toward the end of September. Call 685-0284/685-4768 for details. (If you can't tag along on the day of the trek, do it at your own pace another time. Just ask at any of the major bookstores for the booklet and map prepared for the event by the Civic Heritage Committee.)

The **Greater Vancouver Convention and Visitors Bureau** have designed and published a self-guided walking tour of the downtown, available free at their information stand in Royal Centre Mall (1055 West Georgia, 682-2222). It takes you on a loop through the downtown core, Gastown, Japantown and Chinatown, pointing out historic sites, important buildings, churches, squares and shops. If you just read the little blurbs and look at the landmarks, you can do the whole circuit in about an hour and a half, but you won't really have tasted what the downtown has to offer. Be selective. Take extra time to go in and explore the buildings or areas that twig your curiosity.

If architecture is your thing, pick up Harold Kalman's finely detailed guidebook *Exploring Vancouver 2* in most major bookstores. Kalman charts out six walking tours (including east and west business districts) and four driving tours (including Simon Fraser University) replete with number-keyed maps and photographs of each important building.

Much more general self-guided tours are being marketed by Angus Weller of **Weller Cartographics** (873-9131), but these little pale yellow map/brochures ($1.25) are a bit hard to find. Try Duthie's Books, Woodward's book department or Cara smokeshops. Weller has brochures covering 10 areas, including Stanley Park, Chinatown, Fairview/False Creek, Heritage Homes, Museums & Galleries and a general Sights of Interest map. Text is written by local specialists: Helen Imredy, president of the Vancouver Historical Society, writes about sculpted art in the downtown area; Maritime Museum Curator Leonard McCann writes about the False Creek area; and archivist Paul Yee writes about Chinatown.

Just Kicking Around

If you want to let your own interests and appetites be your guide, be my guest. I happen to be a kicking-around type myself, especially on rainy days when the aroma of steamy espresso seeping out onto the pavement has a way of dissolving my agenda like cocoa powder in hot milk. If you want to see the sights in your own inimitable style, at your own pace, leaving plenty of time to drop into kitchen shops to fiddle with the gadgets, into fashion boutiques to try on something outrageous or into bookstores to wait out a cloudburst, here a few suggestions:

Chinatown

This part of the downtown eastside is so densely packed with people doing commerce, eating, browsing, strolling and cruising (often bumper to bumper) that it is an ideal kick-around destination. You can do it seven days a week (though weekends are most lively), morning, noon or night. You'll get an eyeful whether you're looking into the shops, around at all the people, or up at the turn-of-the-century buildings with their temple-like facades and iron-railed balconies. Second in size on the continent to San Francisco's Chinatown, Vancouver's is the nerve centre of more than 100,000 Chinese living in the

Greater Vancouver area. Give yourself at least two hours to browse through it—longer if you have an appetite.

Probably the best way to see Chinatown is on a guided walking tour organized by the women's committee of the **Chinese Cultural Centre** (687-0729). You should book at least a day ahead to get onto one of these two- to three-hour walkabouts which will take you to cultural points of interest, like the Jin Wah Sing Musical and Opera Society, and into shopping curiosities like the herbalists where they sell dried seahorses and antlers. It costs $8 for the tour, and another $7 if you want to take a guided dim sum lunch at one of the finer Chinatown restaurants. **W.K.Gardens** (687-9608) is a popular choice.

The best starting point is the new **Chinese Cultural Centre**, 50 E. Pender. A Chinatown map/guide is available at the front desk for 50¢, and if there is something special you want to see, the friendly staff will point you in the right direction. In the Cultural Centre's backyard is what promises to be the most beautiful feature of the area, now under construction: The $4 million, 2.5 acre **Dr. Sun Yat-sen Classical Chinese Park and Garden.** Due to open in the fall of 1984, the park will be filled with miniature mountains, pavilions, ponds, bridges and a model of the renowned Ming gardens in Suzhou, Jiangsu province.

East Pender is the heart of Chinatown, so you can't go far wrong simply wandering the two-block stretch from the Cultural Centre east to Gore Street and back. Directly across from your starting point is the *Chinese Times*, at 1 E. Pender, in one of Chinatown's original buildings (1902) which housed the first local Chinese newspaper. You can watch the laborious hand typesetting process through the window: no electronic shortcuts here!

As you wander eastward you pass shop after shop of trinkets, all called So-and-So Trading Co., all crammed full of crafts, souvenirs, silk jackets and slippers, books, records, toys and other exotic junk. But if you become a Chinatown regular you find out they are not all the same. "Most people get used to one shop and they keep coming back," says Tom Liang, owner of **Onward Trading** at 138 E. Pender. Tom, for example, specializes in small items—rice paper fans, cotton shoes, sandalwood soap—and prides himself in having exactly the same stock as he did 15 years ago when he opened. "When people come back they always find the same store." **The Oriental Dragon** (154 E. Pender) has a selection of

CHINATOWN

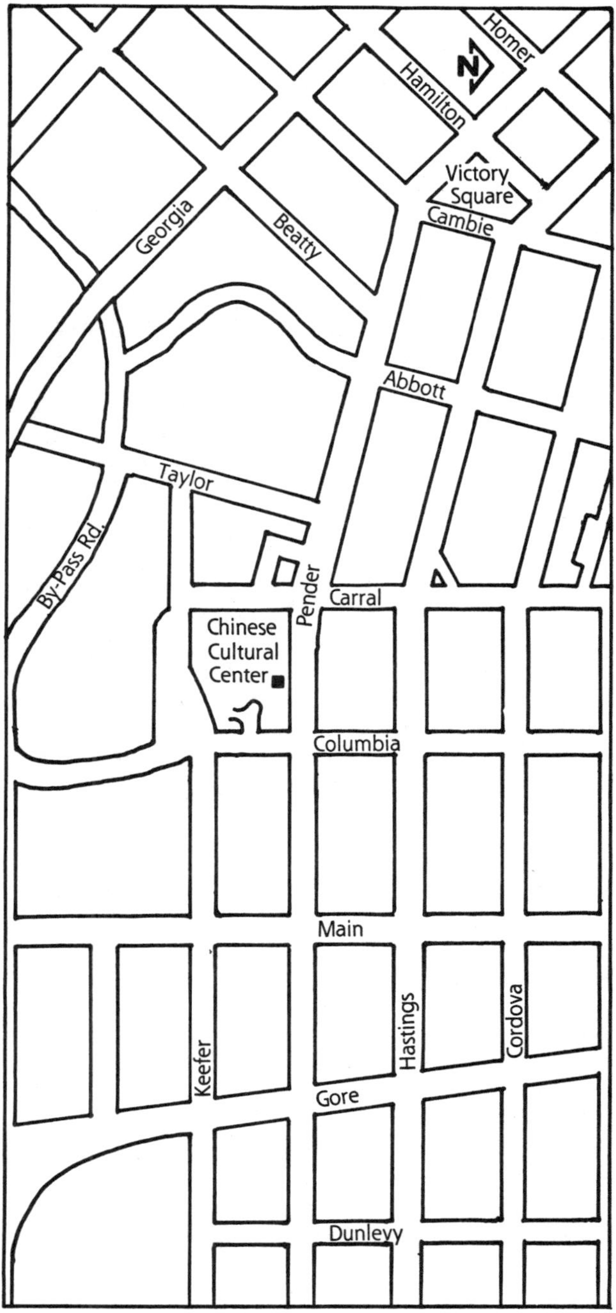
Homer
N
Hamilton
Victory Square
Cambie
Georgia
Beatty
Abbott
Taylor
By-Pass Rd.
Pender
Carral
Chinese Cultural Center
Columbia
Main
Keefer
Hastings
Cordova
Gore
Dunlevy

children's toys you won't find anywhere else, plus a good stock of Chinese records and tapes. Other shops specialize in bamboo articles for the house, others in rice paper hangings and art supplies.

Among the most intriguing shops are the herbalists, with dried seahorses, antler horns, ginseng and exotic teas displayed in the windows. People have been swearing by the power of these herbal medicines for thousands of years. Got a nagging headache? Go in and ask.

There are also classical treasures to be found here. The rosewood antiques and hand-loomed rugs at **Great China Co.** (8 E. Pender) are worth a look; you'll find exquisite Chinese versions of European lutes, hammer dulcimers and flutes at **Perlin Music** (107 E. Pender) and interesting paper art of all kinds from Mainland China at **C.C. Arts Centre** (20 E. Pender). Half a block west, in what Ripley calls the world's narrowest building (8 W. Pender), is one of Vancouver's finest silk shops—**Kuo Kong.** Next door in the same five-foot-wide building is the **Ping Gallery** (12 W. Pender), displaying the fine ceramic pieces of local artists like Wayne Ngan and Sam Kwan.

But let's get down to the real reason most of us go to Chinatown: food. If it's lunchtime, drop into any of the larger restaurants for dim sum. Your best bets for a Chinese dinner are no longer in Chinatown (see Dwelling over Dinner, page 120) but for quick snacks on the go, you can't beat the bakeries, barbecued meat shops and wonton houses along East Pender and Keefer Street, which runs parallel to it a block south.

Sample some barbecued pork or duck (cooked according to a 2,000-year-old tradition and strung along steamy window counters to lure in business); stop by a bakery for a couple of baos for the road (steamed or baked buns stuffed with meat or sweet bean paste); drop into a wonton house for a full meal in a bowl if you want to warm up your insides for under $3; or stock up on fresh ingredients at any of the fresh fish, meat and produce stores along Pender and Gore Streets and cook up your own Chinese feast at home. (If you want to try something different and delicious, take home one of the soya-cured, boned, wind-dried ducks or chickens from **Dollar Meats**, 266 E. Pender, and simply steam it over rice for 25 minutes.)

Getting there: Chinatown is within walking distance of the downtown core, or take the #21 Victoria bus northbound on Granville to Pender at Carrall Street. If you drive, the best parking is in large surface lots on the 100 and 200 blocks Keefer Street.

Commercial Drive

Vancouver's Italian community, numbering more than 50,000, is largely centred in the northeast corner of the city—an area suitably nicknamed Little Italy. Stroll Commercial Drive, from the busy cross-street Venables on the north to East 2nd Ave., and you'll get the picture. In eight blocks, I counted 13 espresso bars. It is an area where you'll find specialty meats like mortatdella at the corner Sub Stop, where you won't find a single Canadian cheddar in the cheese shops, where rather plain looking shoe stores sell $60 kid leather pumps for babies and ice cream parlours always make their own.

Inevitably, Little Italy has been "discovered" by a lot of Big City folks: '60s hippies who couldn't make it back to the land but could get as far as the east end; '70s political types who dug the left-leaning working-class atmosphere; and the late-nesters of the '80s who are trading in their cramped condos for rambling old east end houses fit for kids and pets and handyman hobbies. In short the area isn't really Little Italy any longer, but it still has character. If you start your stroll at Venables, the first few blocks nicely illustrate the point.

The first cafe you pass on the east side is **Il Corsaro** (920), an Italian trattoria from the old school run by the street's most charming old gentleman—Mr. Tessuti. The place is busy, noisy and just a little gaudy with plastic oranges strung from the abundant fig trees. For a startling contrast, Mr. Tessuti's original Il Corsaro a few blocks south (1537) has recently been taken over by restaurant critic and TV personality James Barber who renamed it **Arriva** and rewrote the menu from the traditional spaghetti/chianti combinations to such specialties as "pappardelle verdi al salmone fresco" (green pasta with fresh salmon) and pears in red wine for dessert.

Continuing south from Il Corsaro, you take a little hop around the Mediterranean and land at the **Zagreb Cafe Bar** (1016 Commercial) for baclava and Turkish coffee. Across the street (1045) is one of the most macho espresso bars on the strip—the **Italian Sports Bar,** where sports, presumably, means the pool table and the ubiquitous round of cards going on at the window table. I once saw a woman in there. If the rain is making your kids antsy, **East Side Family Place** is on this block (1034) offering a well-equipped, baby-proof playroom and parents' lounge. There is a nominal drop-in fee (under $1) and you are expected to supervise your child. Maybe this is where the Italian Sports Bar men's women hang out.

La Quena coffee house (1111) takes us deep into the troubled heart of Latin America. It is a political/cultural meeting place, run by the non-profit Canadian-Latin American Culture Society. Drop in for cafe latte, a sandwich and a calendar of events (revolutionary films, folk music from around the world, and poetry readings). The front window is all but blocked with notices, but if you want to take a moment to pore over the most complete noticeboard in the area, cross the street to **Octopus Books East.** Inside is a very good newsstand, well organized selection of used paperbacks and a few records. There is usually something gentle like an old Piaf album playing in the background.

The literati mix with the macho set at espresso bars like the **Continental** a few doors from Octopus, or two blocks further up at the **Pofi Bar** (1308), both of which have window tables ideal for rainy-day sipping and street-watching. You can have cold cuts and cheese sandwiches at these joints, but if you want a more sophisticated nibble, drop into the Portuguese tapas (snack) bar adjoining **Chamine** (1187). It's a favourite of mine, especially since the owner Mr. Santos told me he hand-

COMMERCIAL DRIVE

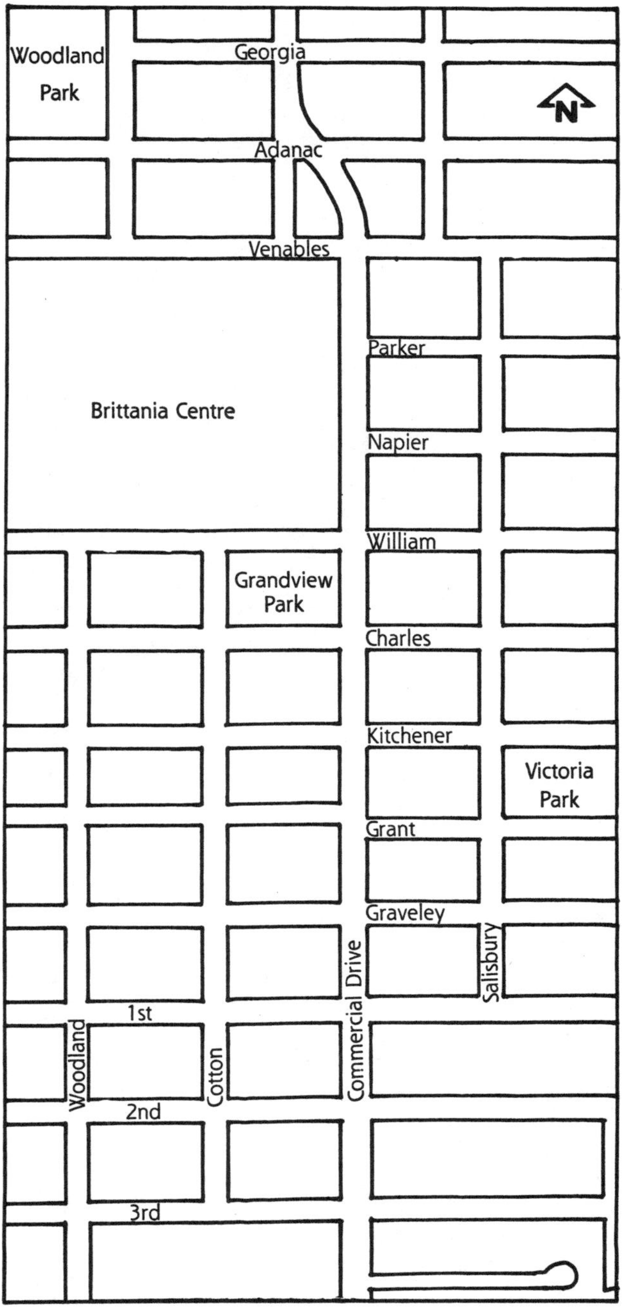

painted all the lovely wall tiles. Stuffed squid is a specialty.

The Italians have a thing for shoes. One of the city's finest shoe stores is **Amorelli,** now in a few locations, but the original is here at 1432. Exquisite and very expensive footwear for the whole family, plus handbags, are unpretentiously displayed. Other fine shoe stores are **Kalena** (1526) and **La Bottega** (1616) specializing in children's shoes as well as imported clothing.

Menswear is serious business here too, and I don't mean the usual off-the-rack fashions. Some of Vancouver's best-dressed men come to tailor shops like **Columbus Five** (1566) and **Angelo's** (1501) where you can also find Italian Vogue lines like Ermenegildo Zegna and Tema Uomo.

You can take a bit of Little Italy home with you with a one-stop shopping spree at the corner of Commercial and 2nd. Giant provolones hanging in the window identify **La Grotta del Formaggio** (1791) where you can buy cheese, spicy sausage, cold cuts, marinated olives, eggplant, and peppers. Also bulk coffee and fresh pasta. If you're into making your own pasta and espresso, **La Ionica** (1789) sells all the machinery. For sweets and crunchy Italian loaves, stop at **Renato's** (1795). For your fresh Italian plum tomatoes, basil, salad vegetables and Concord dessert grapes check out the **Salad Market** just around the corner at 1649 E. 1st.

Walk one-half block west from Commercial along any of the streets we have passed and you come to **Brittania Centre** (1661 Napier), one of Vancouver's finest examples of integrated educational, social and recreational resources: gymansia, ice rink, great pool, public library, teen and retired citizens' centres, and coffee shop.

Getting to Little Italy by bus: Take #21 Victoria from Granville and Georgia St. downtown, heading north. Get off at Commercial and Venables. When to go: any day for the espresso bars and cafes. Any day but Sunday if you want to shop.

Gastown

Let's get it right out in the open: Gastown is a tourist trap. Let's make another thing perfectly clear: I like it. Especially on Sundays when everything is open—and even better, on rainy Sundays when the fake cobblestones glisten under the old-style lamp standards and the famous steam clock looks even prettier through the steamy windows of **La Brasserie de L'Horloge** across the street.

Despite the highly commercial make-over of recent years, Gastown does have quite a history to it. It was the first permanent settlement in the area that was to become Vancouver, named for a sternwheeler captain-turned-hotelier who was nicknamed Gassy Jack Deighton in tribute to his blustery monologue. Gassy Jack's likeness in bronze stands in Maple Tree Square at the intersection of Carrall, Powell, Alexander and Water Streets, where your walk begins. The square is bordered by a good slice of history.

The lovely old flatiron building at 43 Powell is the **Hotel Europe,** the town's most luxurious accommodation in the early part of the century. It is now being redeveloped as an apartment cooperative, due to open in 1985. The other buildings lining the square and continuing on down Water Street are beautifully renovated and mostly filled with gift boutiques, galleries (see Art Tour, page 47) and restaurants. One of the notable buildings, still on the square is the **Byrnes Block** (2 Water St.) which was built in 1886 and housed one of Gassy Jack's saloons. You can tell by the ornate window pediments, pilasters and decorated cornice that the original Alhambra Hotel, upstairs, was no fleabag hotel. It charged more than a dollar a night! Newer tenants in the building include the delightful fabric and fashion boutique **Laura Ashley,** a very fragrant gift shop called **Soaps & Scents, Guenter's Deli Restaurant** offering hearty soups and sandwiches either indoors or at sidewalk tables, and a **Baskin-Robbins** ice cream parlour. Gastown goes on like that for about eight blocks. Try kicking around it in the following loop.

Head down Water Street westward, past the **Gastown Wax Museum** (on the corner of Water and Alexander), past the delightful **Antique Hypermarket** (24 Water), past my very favourite contemporary furnishings store, **Inform Interiors** (97), and on to the area's only really modern shopping complex, **Gaslight Square** (131). Fortunately this development is tastefully in synch with the old architecture—bay windows, brick facades, awnings and all. Among the worthwhile shops in it is a sweet little children's boutique called **No More Twist** where owner/designer Gerri Schelini produces and sells her distinctive Viyella pinafores and taffeta party dresses.

You'll soon encounter the steam clock at the corner of Cambie and Water, wheezing out something akin to a tune on the quarter hour. Take note of the beautifully redeveloped warehouses along this 300 block, now housing (what else?) boutiques downstairs, some very chic and lofty offices upstairs, and the area's most notable restaurant down a narrow hallway—**Al Porto di Umberto** (321 Water, 683-8376), a chic pasta trattoria run by the king of Vancouver's Italian cuisine, Umberto Menghi (more in Dwelling over Dinner, page 122). Kitty-corner is the newest commercial redevelopment, **Le Magasin** (332) housing some exclusive gift/fashion boutiques on two levels: **Soulieado** for printed cottons from Provence; **Fogal of Switzerland** for hosiery and lingerie; **Green & Piehl Goldsmiths;** an irresistible chocolate shop called **Tout Sweet; Galipots** for gifts; a wonderfully stocked newsstand and **The Restaurant at Le Magasin** (687-1029) where you must try the souffle (see page 115).

To close the loop around Gastown, take the very pointy corner at Cordova, check out the curiosity shops and new-wavish used clothes boutiques as you stroll Cordova back to Carrall, then up to Maple Tree Square for a much needed coffee, ice cream and chat with Gassy Jack.

Getting to Gastown: It is a short walk from downtown, and easy to find because it lies in the shadow of the Harbour Centre tower. You might want to start your tour of Gastown with a view stop at the Harbour Centre observation deck (see page 7), then walk the short block down Cordova to the intersection with Water St. You are now on the west edge of Gastown, so you can do the loop backwards. If you're coming by bus, take #50 False Creek South running north along Granville St. all the way to Water St., or #3 Main, #6 Fraser or #12 Powell north on Granville to Cordova, then walk north a block to Water.

The West End

The western half of the downtown peninsula, bounded by Burrard St. on the east, Stanley Park on the west, Robson St. on the north and English Bay on the south, is one of the most attractive pieces of core city land in North America. That's why strolling through it is a fascinating study in urban density. Its main arteries (Burrard, Robson, Davie, Denman) are packed with more boutiques, cafes, hotels, convenience stores, ice cream parlours and croissant shops than you can shake your umbrella at, and the residential area (virtually everything in between) boasts more people per square foot than does any North American neighborhood outside of Manhattan.

It's a fine area for umbrella touring, especially along the shopping streets where awnings provide plenty of cover. If it's not too blustery, do take a wander through the residential streets where trees provide only partial cover. The level grade of the streets and profusion of landscaped mini-parks in the residential area make this an ideal stroll for older people. Also, you will encounter a good number of other seniors on your way, as some 20,000 of them live in the West End. You can wander as the spirit moves you, or take the following route for an interesting mix of sights.

Because the West End is part of the downtown core, you can start or end your tour with a visit to one of the downtown landmarks. For a bit of culture, take in the **Vancouver Art Gallery** situated in the magnificently restored old courthouse building at Robson and Hornby. A block away on Burrard is the Chateau-style **Hotel Vancouver,** built cooperatively 50 years ago by the Canadian National and Canadian Pacific Railways. (To find it from anywhere in the area just look up and you'll see its copper-green roof). There is a comfortable lounge in the gracious old lobby. For a stop of religious/historical interest, there is **Christ Church Cathedral** across the street at 690 Burrard. This is Vancouver's oldest surviving church, the granite basement constructed in 1888 and the rest six years later. The Tudor-style building, with its striking Douglas fir roof and stained-glass windows, came a breath away from the wrecker's ball in 1973 when city council vetoed a developer's plan to replace it with an office tower. (Whew!) You can take a guided 30-minute tour Sundays if you book in advance: 682-3848.

Head south down Burrard one block to Robson and you're at the north border of the West End—a colourful and always busy shopping street. Proceed westward as your curiosity and pocketbook dictate. Try to walk this stretch at mealtime, or at the very least snacktime, or you will miss some great opportunities. Even if you are positively stuffed, I dare you to walk past **Ping Pong** (Italian ice cream parlour, 1129), **Daniel's Le Chocolat**

WEST END

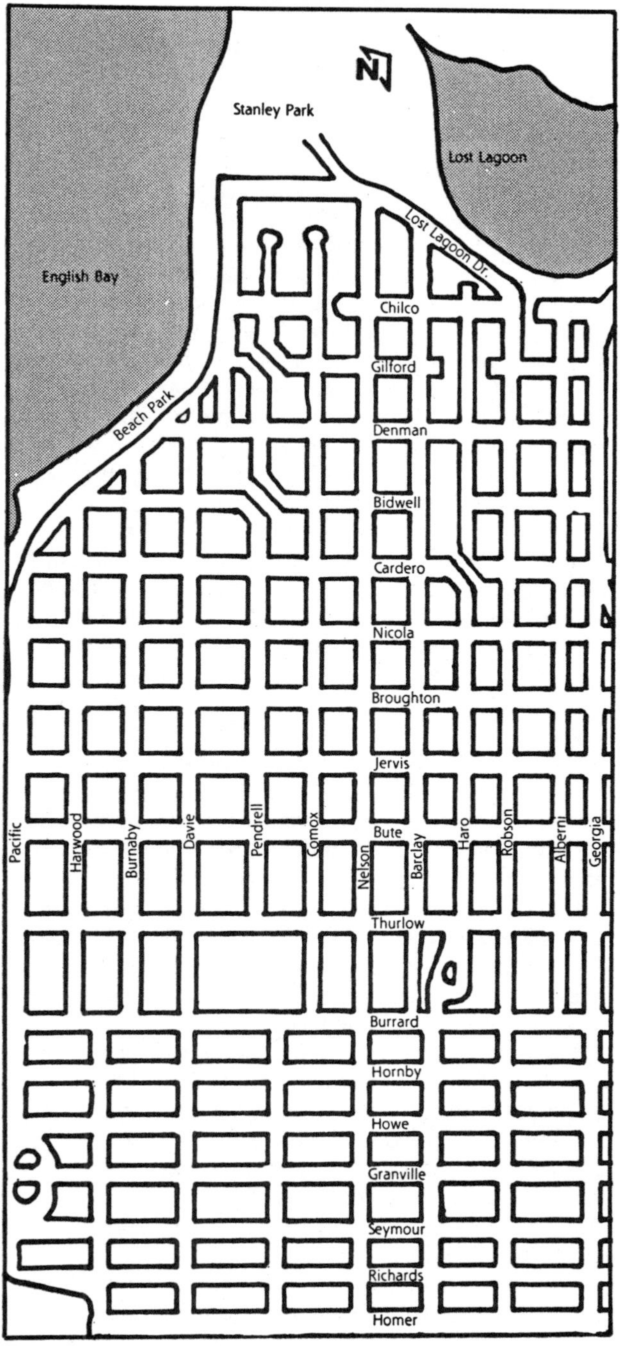
Stanley Park
N
Lost Lagoon
Lost Lagoon Dr.
English Bay
Beach Park
Chilco
Gilford
Denman
Bidwell
Cardero
Nicola
Broughton
Jervis
Bute
Thurlow
Burrard
Hornby
Howe
Granville
Seymour
Richards
Homer
Pacific
Harwood
Burnaby
Davie
Pendrell
Comox
Nelson
Barclay
Haro
Robson
Alberni
Georgia

Belge (1133) or **The Gourmet Croissant** (1135) without breaking down and buying a sweet nosh.

It is just two blocks to Bute St., a good place to turn left and head into the residential area. If you are cheating and doing this tour in a car, don't even bother trying to proceed through here. The city has created a nightmarish maze of one-way streets, deadends, barriers and streetcorner pedestrian parks to dissuade motorists from ruining the peace of the neighborhood. They say cars have entered the maze and never reappeared.

Follow Bute through the pedestrian-park intersection with Haro, two blocks further to the larger cross-street Nelson, noting as you go the vintage 1910-1920 brick apartment buildings nestled among the boxy three-storey walk-ups of the '50s and the towers of the '60s and '70s. The mid-century was not a high period for living aesthetics, though it was certainly high on density. During the late '50s and early '60s the old West End, its gabled wooden houses and dignified apartment-hotels, was all but obliterated by a forest of high-rises. Fortunately City Council, trying to undo some of the damage in recent years, has created tiny parks where you least expect them, allowed developers to reach skyward only if they keep their buildings pencil thin, and encouraged low-rise townhouse construction on scale with the area's few remaining houses. Look around when you reach the intersection of Nelson and Bute—thin new towers to the left, new condos to the right, boxes dead ahead.

Turn right on Nelson, go two blocks to Broughton and turn left, continuing down through the mini-park, past the lovely reconstruction of **St. John's United Church,** noting one of those original Tudor-style three-storey walk-ups at 1100 Broughton. Turn right there onto Pendrell, proceed one block to Nicola, then left one more to Davie Street where you will see, on your right, a beautifully renovated mansion-cum-steakhouse. It's called **Gabriola** because it is built of stone brought in from Gabriola Island in the Georgia Strait. Leading residential architect of the day, Samuel Maclure, built it in 1900 for sugar magnate B.T. Rogers and it remains a potent reminder of the West End's grand era before everyone who was anyone packed and moved to Shaughnessy. Walk on past the mansion, a few short blocks to the intersection of Davie and Denman. Once here, you have a dozen options for the remainder of your tour.

You can call it a day and take a cab or the #1 Beach bus back along scenic Beach and Pacific Avenues to

Burrard; you can walk the beach route along the seawall, braving the wet wind off the bay while savouring one of the city's most spectacular views; you can take a sharp turn north on Denman and browse along six more blocks of boutiques till you get back to Robson; you can turn your collar against the elements and trek straight through to Stanley Park (details page 40); or you can pack it in and stay put for an hour or two in one of the English Bay area's many cafes and watering holes.

A few recommendations: **The English Bay Cafe** (1795 Beach, 669-2225) is the old-time favourite, with a very comfortable lounge offering light snacks on the first floor and a fairly pricey but gracious dining room upstairs—both levels offer picture-postcard views. One of the best quick snack stops in the city is right across the street—called simply **Souvlaki** (no phone) and guess what they serve? Probably the best, drippiest, tangiest pita-full of grilled meats and salads that you can get outside of the Greek strip of West Broadway. If cappuccino, pastry or frozen yogurt with fruit appeals, drop into the **Rialto Gelateria** (855 Denman, 681-1500).

Getting there by bus: #5 Robson takes you straight to Davie and Denman from Burrard, and the #1 Beach gets you back the scenic way. When to go: Almost all Robson and Denman shops are open Sundays, so you can do this tour plus some serious shopping any day of the week.

South Granville and Shaughnessy Crescent

Here's a walk for people who either have a fistful of money to spend or who like to imagine what they'd do with it if they had it. South Granville is the kind of shopping street people go to in order to avoid rubbing shoulders with the proles downtown; The Crescent is the kind of street you live on if you're married to a Supreme Court judge or your grandfather owns major chunks of B.C.'s forestland—preferably both.

It's called South Granville not because it is in the south end of the city, but because it lies on that side of the Granville St. Bridge, across from downtown. Our kick-around tour begins at the foot of the bridge, at Granville and 6th which is dominated by the Pacific Press Building, home of *The Vancouver Sun* and *The Province*. (That's right: two competing daily newspapers under the same roof, majority owned by the same company. Picture the rival reporters munching sandwiches across the table from one another in the same cafeteria and then racing out to scoop the day's story first.)

THE CRESCENT

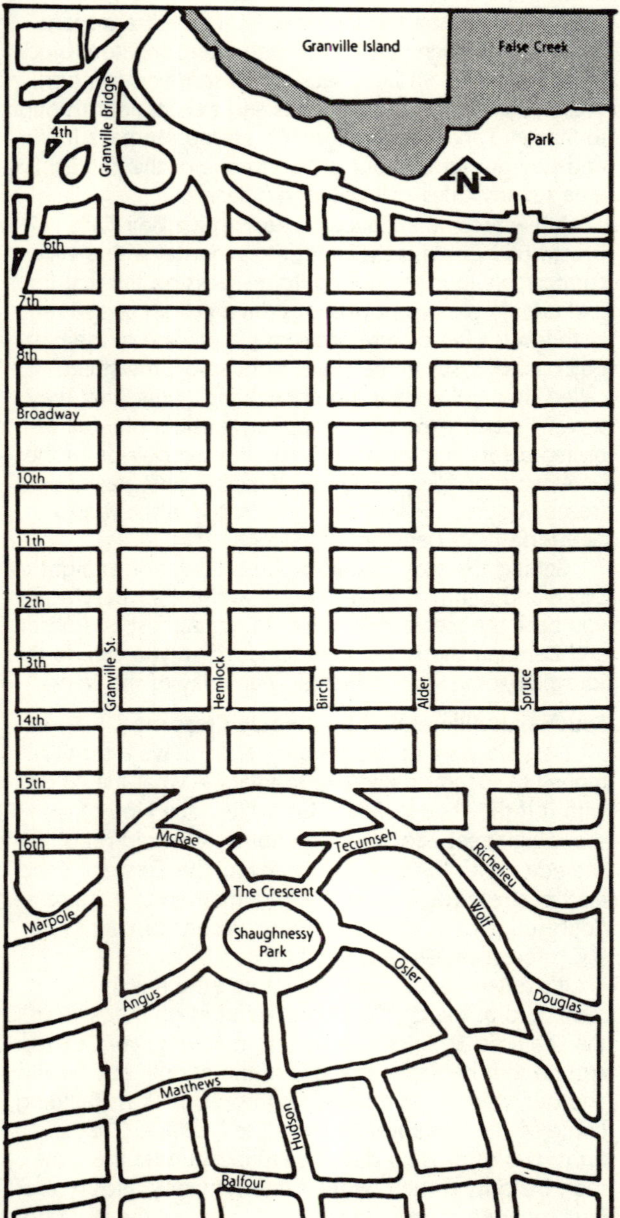

The 10-block stretch of specialty shops, art galleries and cafes on Granville between 6th and 16th is amply endowed with awnings and inviting places to duck into when the wind whips the water at you despite the cover. It is an ideal window-shopping street for all ages thanks to the relatively flat grade of the street (especially south of Broadway) and the surprising variety of its tenants. Older folks will appreciate shops that cater to the many seniors living in nearby apartments, and younger ones will enjoy browsing through some of Vancouver's most trendy boutiques. Art lovers will also find plenty of interest (see Art Tour, page 44).

The main emphasis in the three blocks from 6th to Broadway is household goods. Even though my budget is limited, I always pay a visit to the colourful and quirky **Industrial Revolution** (2306) where you can find plastic wine glasses for picnics next to high-tech Italian kitchen cupboards and gold-plated straight razors. Nearby is the city's finest wicker shop, **Malacca Rattan** (2301) where you can also find upholstery fabrics and an unusual selection of cloth, paper and dried flowers. A block south is one of Vancouver's most highly reputed oriental rug dealers, **Shindler & Co.** (2415). But if you are in the market for decorative rugs, don't make any hasty decisions. There are close to a dozen rug specialists on South Granville. Shop around.

As we proceed southward from Broadway, the emphasis shifts to high-fashion clothing. There are more worthwhile shops than I can list, but among the truly exceptional are:

- Women's fashions: **Bacci** (1495 West 12) for the trendiest and most expensive from Italy; **Edward Chapman** (2596) for the conservative British look; **Speiser's** (2706) for furs; **Freedman's** (2867) for shoes; **Tickles** (2572) for lingerie; **Saba's** (2556) or **Farquahar's** (2762) for fabrics; **Suki's** (2997) for hair.
- Men's fashions: **Numero Uno** (2820) for Italian imports straight out of Vogue.
- Children's: **Baby Boom** (10th and Granville) for nifty gifts; **Bratz** (2828) for Vogue Bambini; **Kinderspel** (3039) for toys.

If you are hungry, you can start your walk with a hearty meal of pork tortiere and maple sugar pie at **La Quebecoise** (2537 Granville, 733-5522)—an intimate lunch/dinner spot that especially appeals to visitors from south of the border who never considered that Quebec might have its own distinctive cuisine. Moderately expensive. If a lighter meal is in order, your choices are too numerous to list. My favourite few are: the **Vegetable Patch** (1484 West Broadway, 738-5233) for all things fresh and healthy: **Szasz** (2881 Granville, 738-7922) for a steaming bowl of Hungarian goulash soup; **Polly's** (2977 Granville, 734-4466) for a stuffed croissant and tea.

How comfortable are your walking shoes? How wet are your socks? If you still have the energy and interest, one of the most exquisite house tours in Canada is a short hill-climb away.

On the southeast corner of Granville and 16th you will see a narrow street angling up a forested hill—it is McRae Ave., the approach to **The Crescent,** the hub of Old

Shaughnessy. Here the city's most influential families moved during the first two decades of the century to get clear of the creeping density of downtown's West End. It was getting downright impossible to keep an acre for yourself down there. But up on the hill, Canadian Pacific Railway was generously carving up its land holdings to create an exclusive neighborhood, designed by a romantic Danish engineer and a Montreal landscape architect who envisioned something akin to New York's Central Park and Montreal's Mount Royal: tree-lined streets and wide boulevards curving along the natural contours of the land.

The Crescent is a circle of 14 massive homes with a lush boulevard park in the middle—a mere stone's throw from the busy intersection of 16th and Granville, but a continent away in mood. Rolls Royces creep silently round the circle carrying children from Crofton House school or old ladies from tea at the Shaughnessy Heights Golf Club. Back behind graceful hedges and cobbled driveways lie houses that never change, that never even betray signs of life inside. (Twelve of the 14 are not allowed to change by city ordinance. They have special "Heritage" designation, and you will understand why when you see them.) Here are a few fine examples:

McRae House, or Hycroft (1489 McRae) is on your left as you walk up from Granville. The facade of this 75-year-old mansion is dominated by six massive columns supporting a classical porte-cochere. The beautifully restored interior includes a grand ballroom, now used chiefly by the University Women's Club, which calls Hycroft its home. On your right as you approach The Crescent is the **Walter C. Nichol House** (1402 The Crescent), a 1912 trend-setter in Shaughnessy as the first of many Tudor Revivals. It was built for Province newspaper publisher Nichol, later to become a B.C. Lieutenant-Governor, by architect Samuel Maclure who is credited with some of British Columbia's finest buildings of the day.

Swinging left around The Crescent (clockwise) we come to the **Henry M. Leggat House** (1363), built in 1911 in the style of an 18th Century New England Georgian townhouse—large porches, shuttered sash windows and all. **Villa Russe** (3390 Osler) is a sharp contrast in style, built in 1921 for Russian emigree Misak Y. Aivazoff who hosted a steady stream of Russian artists and nobility. If you want a short walk, continue round the circle past the Classical Revival house of **George E.**

MacDonald (1350) which boasts Ionic capitals, Roman pediments and Renaissance "Paladian" windows; go on past the Dutch Colonial Revival house of **Frederick M. Kelly** (1398) and then back down McRae to Granville. If you're up for a longer stroll, leave The Crescent at Villa Russe, heading down Osler Street where you will soon encounter the **Frank L. Buckley House** (3498 Osler) on your left. Built in 1913 for a lumber magnate, this fine Gothic/Classical house was used as the Russian consulate in the movie *Russian Roulette.*

Gore-Tex and Gumboot Tours

In this city, plants get equal billing with people. Before there was Vancouver, there was rain forest, which I guess explains our fixation with the great wet outdoors: We're guilty for having paved over the mossy forest floor in the name of civilization, so we spend a good deal of energy trying to put the rain forest back into our lives. We putter in our gardens all year round, we fill our homes with plants, and take walks through perennially green parks and forests rain or shine. For brevity, I have chosen five great walks to share with you.

Reifel Migratory Bird Sanctuary

This walk is a family favourite thanks to our toddler's predilection for all things winged. If you have one such in your family, toss him, his back-pack carrier and plenty of warm clothes into the car and drive down to this remote piece of marshland at the mouth of the Fraser River near Ladner. Best time to trek the marshes is November through March when more than 250 species of wildfowl will keep you company—Canada geese, snow geese, crazy coots (watch them walk on water!) and just plain "birdies" that were heading south for the winter when they spotted this place and decided to touch down here instead. The park office, run by the **B.C. Waterfowl Society** (946-6980), supplies seed packets and free trail-guide pamphlets to turn your walk into a self-guided nature tour.

You can casually wander or seriously walk here, taking advantage of well maintained and generally dry trails along dykes sheltered by shore pine, Douglas fir and alder. If it is raining hard you had best avoid the treeless dykes along Roberts Bank where the six-foot growth of cattail and grass crowding the walkway will leave you wishing you, too, had webbed feet. Those who brave it through this wild wetness arrive at an observation platform from which you can view the whole tidal area plus, if you are lucky, one or two of the elusive great blue herons lurking in the outer marsh.

Admission to the sanctuary is $2.50 adults, $1 children/seniors. It is open 9 a.m. to 5 p.m., no one admitted after 4 p.m. You get there by car (no public transit available) on Hwy 99 south to the Victoria Ferry turnoff, right to the first lights, right again through the town of Ladner. The road you're on changes names a few times before becoming River Road West which, in about two miles, leads you onto a bridge to Westham Island and directly to the park entrance. If you have no car, read on. The next four destinations are serviced by buses.

Capilano Canyon

Go to Capilano Canyon in the rain: you will find yourself pretty much alone to savour the awesome contrast between tiny man and monumental nature. I'm talking about the experience of inching your way across the seemingly fragile rope-and-wood suspension bridge that stretches 135 metres across the canyon, 70 metres (25 storeys) above the Capilano River. It is one of Vancouver's major tourist attractions, so on sunny days you can count on sharing the experience with kids skipping and leaping fearlessly across the bridge, shrieking with laughter as the undulations turn your knuckles white and your complexion green.

Rain or shine, the view from the bridge is truly special. Towering Douglas firs and cedars line the canyon walls; speck-sized people can be seen strolling the trail that weaves through the forest, around ponds and through the mist of a 60-metre waterfall; and in the months of July through October the river beneath you will appear a shimmering reddish mass of bank-to-bank salmon as the spawning Coho and Chinook make their way upstream to the **Capilano Salmon Hatchery** (see Nature Under Cover, page 92).

Canyon climbing is made relatively easy thanks to well designed trails and steps in the steepest areas. Heavy-tread walking shoes or boots are advised for traction. But if clambering makes you nervous, stick to the high-elevation trail (half an hour is all you'll need for a scenic loop through the woods). Make a stop en route to the parking lot at the **Trading Post** which is stocked with a better selection of Indian artifacts and knick-knacks than you'll find anywhere else.

To get to the canyon: drive across the Lions Gate Bridge to Marine Drive East, left on Capilano Rd. for 3 km.; or take the #246 Highland bus west on Georgia St.

downtown and get off at Ridgewood and Capilano Rd. Contact any of the tourist information offices for regularly scheduled bus tours. Open daily, 8 a.m. to dark in summer; 8:15 a.m. to 5 p.m. in winter. Admission $2.75 adults, $2 students and seniors, $1 children 6 to 12 years (985-7474).

Nitobe Gardens

Local gardening is marked by a strong Japanese influence, highlighted by bonsai pruning, intricate rock formations, proliferation of ornamental trees, cherry blossoms, and carp. If you like that sort of thing, you will love the **Nitobe Memorial Gardens,** just west of the Anthropology Museum on Chancellor Blvd. at University of B.C. (228-3928). Many a tormented student has wandered these serene paths and decided against taking the plunge from the Point Grey cliffs. The tranquil perfection of this circular garden filled with exotic plants, ponds stocked with goldfish, a stream filled with carp, stone snowlanterns and an authentic ceremonial teahouse, has an impact that far surpasses its small size. You can wander through the entire garden in 20 minutes, or dwell in it for hours.

Early spring when the air is filled with the intoxicating fragrance of hundreds of cherry blossom trees in full bloom is the best time to visit. But even in the dead of winter, when the stones are covered in wet moss and (even better) the shrubbery is dusted with snow, these gardens are enchanted. When you shut your eyes, you can almost hear the sound of one hand clapping. Dedicated to renowned humanitarian Dr. Inazo Nitobe, the gardens are operated by Friends of the Garden, a volunteer group that offers guided tours; book two weeks in advance by calling 228-3928. Open daily 10 a.m. to 30 minutes before sunset from Easter to Thanksgiving, to 3 p.m. weekdays only in winter. Nominal admission fee.

Getting there: drive west on 4th, veering left up the hill where it forks at Jericho Park, continuing as it turns into Chancellor Blvd. Turn right into the Botanical Gardens parking area. By bus: take #10 Tenth - U.B.C. south from Granville St. downtown, terminating at a shelter with a campus map pointing the way (very near) to the gardens.

Stanley Park

This 1,000-acre mid-town park is probably the best known, most thoroughly explored and enjoyed piece of greenery in Canada. I considered leaving it out of the book, but that would be like the Bible without Creation. It figures high in my best-wet-walks list, chiefly because the 9 km. seawall walk (crowded as it is, rain or shine) affords one of the best water-level views in the city. Also, there are lots of good places to eat in and near the park, and there are dozens of things you can do on each visit to differentiate it from your last. The big draws are the aquarium (see Nature Under Cover, page 90) and the zoo (see Playing With Kids, page 67).

My favourite walk skirts the west edge of the park, starting at the Beach Ave. entrance on English Bay. If you can find the courage to tear your eyes away from the maniacal rollerskaters streaking past and the tandem cyclists weaving dangerously in and out of their bike lane, you will notice the beautiful log-strewn beaches, dense fir and cedar forests and rolling lawns on either side of the seawall. Between Second and Third Beaches is the park's best playground for kids. Further along, where dripping, moss-clad cliffs rise on your right, you will see the strangely formed Siwash Rock to your left, often crowned with a slender, crested cormorant plotting his flight path from this craggy perch.

As you round the seawall's northern tip, under the Lions Gate Bridge, your view changes to the bustling harbour traffic and north shore mountains beyond. By now you've been walking at least an hour, and if you are good for another two, continue along the seawall for a swing around the park's east edge to Coal Harbour and Lost Lagoon, bird-feeding capital of the West Coast. If you've seen enough of the seawall, cut through the park at the Beaver Lake sign just past the Lions Gate. The trail, well sheltered by forest, takes you into some of the quieter reaches of Stanley Park and around this over-grown lake where you won't see a single beaver but you may spot a great blue heron. The trail takes you back out by way of Lost Lagoon where you'll see many varieties of birds and marine life, including Canada geese and the rare trumpeter swan. For more park information, 681-1141. Bus access: #11 Stanley Park west on Pender. By car: drive west along Beach Ave. or Georgia until you run into it.

False Creek & Granville Island

Here is an urban walk that gets more urban, and more interesting, every day. The flats around False Creek bordering the downtown peninsula on the south were nothing but industrial slums a decade ago. The city, in one of its most insightful and ambitious moments, decided to redevelop the area, dividing it into graceful parcels of medium-density residential zoning, richly landscaped parkland and just enough commecial space to offer strollers a reward of cappuccino or beer if they make it all the way from one corner of the creek to the other. About 4,000 people live on the south shore now, in a mixture of luxury townhouses, co-op apartments, seniors' residences and specially equipped homes for the disabled. Within the next 10 years, another 30,000 are expected to move into homes around the creek, most of them in high-density apartments planned for the north shore adjacent to the **Expo 86** site. The furious level of construction, including some truly monstrous forms emerging in the Expo site, make for interesting walk-talk.

I like to start my False Creek walk at the northeast end, Stamp's Landing, heading west for a round-about on **Granville Island** at lunchtime, then back to car or bus at the east parking area just off 6th Ave. This walk can take a couple of hours or half a day.

There is not much shelter along the False Creek seawall, but the seawall stretches are short and you are always a five-minute sprint from cafes, shops or the Granville Island markets (produce, marine equipment, crafts). From the produce market you have to leave the seawall to get around the Ocean Cement yards, then head back to the water via the open-air mall in the **Emily Carr College of Art** where you can see students' work in progress. Just east of the college is **Sea Village,** Canada's poshest floating homes community. As you round the east tip of Granville Island, heading back toward the False Creek residential area, you pass the indoor/outdoor restaurants of the **Granville Island Hotel,** for anyone who loves to be surrounded by beautiful views and beautiful people. (See also Lingering Over Lunch, page 112.)

To get there by car: turn off West 6th at the lights near Heather St., veering right toward the Stamps Landing parking lot. By bus: take #50 False Creek South at any Granville St. stop downtown, heading south.

FALSE CREEK

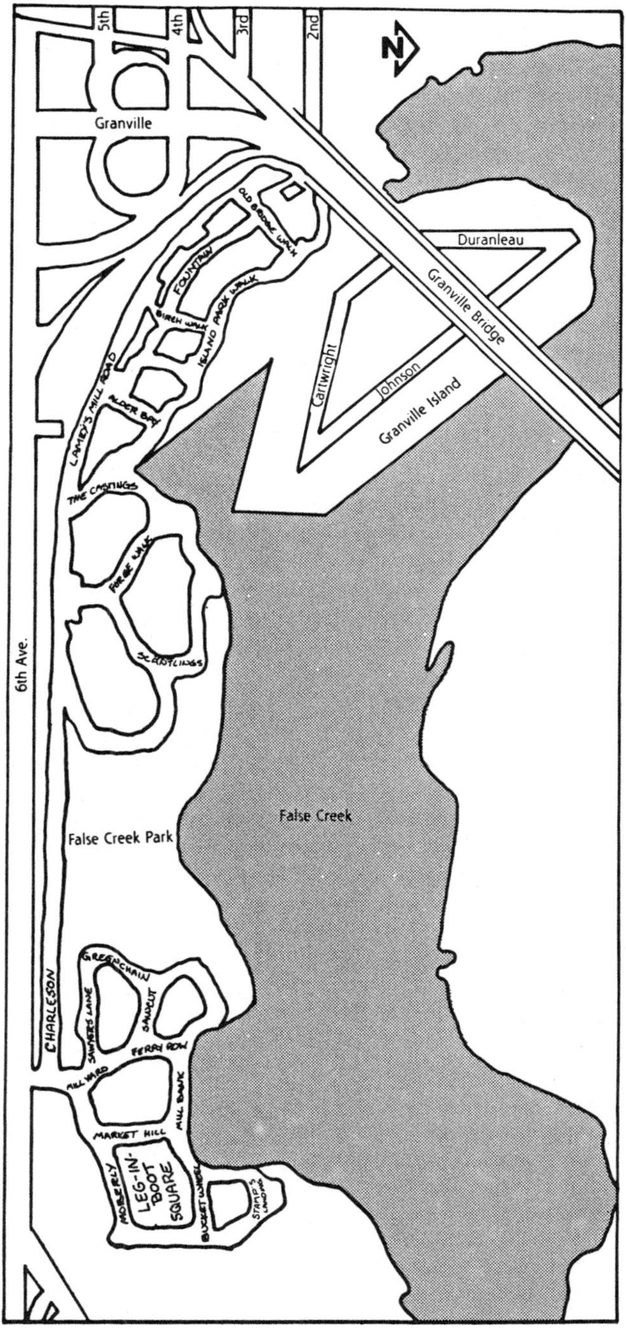

5th
4th
3rd
2nd
N
Granville
Old Bridge Walk
Fountain
Island Park Walk
Birch Walk
Lamey's Mill Road
Alder Bay
Duranleau
Granville Bridge
Cartwright
Johnson
Granville Island
The Castings
Forge Walk
Scantlings
6th Ave.
False Creek
False Creek Park
Greenchain
Sawyers Lane
Sawcut
Charleson
Ferry Row
Mill Yard
Mill Bank
Market Hill
Moberly
Leg-in-Boot Square
Bucket Wheel
Stamp's Landing

GET CULTURAL

Art Tour

Vancouver art galleries seem to crop up in clusters, which is rather convenient when it comes to rainy-day art touring. By selecting a neighbourhood, you can explore a great number and variety of galleries. Because distance between galleries is rarely more than a five-minute stroll, often under cover of awnings, there is no better solution to the rainy-day blahs than a quick and colourful escape onto canvas. Just one word of advice. Wherever you decide to tour, start or finish with a stop at the Vancouver Art Gallery, now located in the gorgeously renovated Robson Square Courthouse. (If you want a really thorough current listing of local galleries, pick up VAG's *Vanguard* magazine, available at the VAG bookstore and other major shops.)

Vancouver Art Gallery

Vancouver's leading architect Arthur Erickson has transformed the courtrooms, judges' chambers, sheriffs' offices and long, dark corridors of the Courthouse into four gleaming white, skylit storeys of exhibit space for the **Vancouver Art Gallery's** (682-5621) permanent and visiting collections. Included in the permanent: Thomas Gainsborough, Francisco Goya, Georges Braque, Pablo Picasso, John Constable, Marc Chagall and a selection of Canadian classics by The Group of Seven. Future exhibitors include the best of contemporary American art, treasures of the Orient (spring 1985) and retrospectives of leading Canadians such as Alex Colville (summer 1984).

My favourite room, apart from the restaurant which overlooks the sculpture garden, is the **Emily Carr Gallery.** It houses the 157 paintings and drawings she bequeathed to the people of B.C., supplemented by private donations which make this an unrivalled tribute to the mystical interpreter of our coastal rain forests and the native people who inhabited them in the early part of the century. Books on Emily Carr and reproductions of her art are on sale in the Gallery Shop off the main entrance, where you will find the best selection of general art books and posters in the town. (For the Children's Gallery at VAG: see Kid Culture, page 75.)

South Granville St.

The greatest concentration of private galleries is on this 10-block strip of Granville Street just over the bridge from downtown. Between 6th and 16th there are more than a dozen galleries, ranging from high-priced contemporary classic to off-beat alternative, Native Indian to English Period art. The many cafes and restaurants along the way make all the difference between a serious art trek and a pleasant art tour. The following is just a sampling of the best galleries, starting at 6th and Granville.

Robertsbridge (2227) is a sombre little place run by serious people with a thorough knowledge of 18th, 19th and early 20th century English paintings. Owner Anthony Chick edits the journal *Art & Antiques* which you can pick up here as a guide to the whole city scene. **Kupczynski Studio Gallery** (2233) is just as it sounds— homebase for Stanley and Eva Kupczynski who paint bright coloured, idyllic scenes of pretend animals, crazy musicians and saucer-eyed children surrounded by fields of flowers. Innocent art for a sophisticated, and growing, clientele. **Kenneth Heffel Fine Art** (2247) houses probably the most prestigious private exhibition of the Group of Seven and their Canadian contemporaries. More moderate priced paintings and drawings can be found in Heffel's second salon featuring mainly contemporary B.C. artists.

Continuing south to 8th and turning right a few steps,

you arrive at **Equinox Gallery** (1525 West 8th) where a number of Vancouver's prominent artists got their start; Bill Reid, Gathy Falk, Robert Michener and Takao Tanabe have had major shows here. There is also a decent selection of prints by contemporary Americans. Further up Granville are two of Vancouver's more established (read conservative) galleries—**Art Emporium** (2928) and **Alexander Harrison Gallery** (2932), running the gamut from Canadian classic to local marine paintings. We swing to the modern side on the next block, with **Atelier Gallery** (3039) specializing in contemporary young Canadians like Richard Davis and Les Graff, and the **Bau-Xi** (3045) which has earned a national reputation for introducing important new artists; among the accomplished artists displayed here are Jack Shadbolt and Allister Bell. Just around the corner at 15th is a must-stop for anyone interested in Indian art, **The Bent-Box Gallery** (1520 West 15th) featuring fine contemporary examples of Northwest Coast art, including limited-edition serigraphs, wood carvings and silver pieces.

If you want to decorate your entire interior and not just the walls, you are on the right street. Oriental rug shops abound on Granville, as well as some of the best antique galleries. Worth noting are **Uno Langmann Antiques** (2117) for European classics, **Frankie Robinson Antiques** (1527 West 10th) for Oriental treasures, and **Copper Kettle** (2331), **Arkay** (3040), **Deelers** (3055) and **Hampshire Antiques** (3149) for quality and wide variety.

Granville Island

The **Emily Carr College of Art** is here, providing a young, vibrant nucleus for this artsy-craftsy community. Just right of the main entrance is the small but very well run **Charles H. Scott Gallery,** showing generally avant-garde works of national repute. On Cartwright St. are two galleries dedicated to the ceramic and textile arts: **The Cartwright Street Gallery** (1411) is publicly subsidized and therefore able to show sometimes esoteric, often exquisite, collections of nationally known art, while the more commercial **Pot Shop and Gallery** (1359) sticks with moderate-priced ceramics.

Above **Malaspina Printmakers** (1555 Duranleau St.) where you can watch the printmaking process in action through plate glass, is **Six of One Gallery** cooperatively run by six artists who do their drawing, etching and printmaking on the premises. They also exhibit the work of underexposed local artists, but they're open odd hours—usually Saturday, Sunday, Tuesday and Thursday afternoons. Also worth a look on Granville Island are the **Creekhouse Gallery** (1551 Johnston) specializing in marine and landscape paintings, and **Granville Island Graphics** (1650 Johnston) offering limited-edition original prints of Canadian and local artists, including Tony Onley and Alexandra Dikeaos.

Gastown & Chinatown

As far as serious art goes, it's slim pickings down here in Gastown where wonderful old buildings that cry out for fine art are jammed with dime-store souvenirs. Of the few worthwhile galleries, my favourite gift stop is **Circle Craft Co-op** (348 Water St.) where you won't find collectible art but you will find neat, sometimes bizarre creations of wool, wood or clay. Also on Water Street: **Federation Gallery** (367) is home of the Federation of Canadian Artists, offering rapidly changing exhibits of some of Vancouver's leading artists—Sam Black, Daniel Izzard and George Bates among them; **Inuit Gallery** (345) has one of Vancouver's largest collection of native carvings, drawings and prints. Around the corner at **Coburg Gallery** (314 West Cordova) the work of local photographers is featured in monthly shows.

You can walk or drive the few blocks to the galleries of Chinatown and Japantown. It's not just the rice-paper paintings and inlaid wooden screens that you might expect in this part of town. At **Ping Gallery** in "the narrowest building in the world" (12 West Pender) you will find some of the city's finest ceramic art, notably by Wayne Ngan and Sam Kwan. For a stark contrast, **Unit Pitt Gallery** (163 West Pender) is a thriving alterntive art centre featuring the mixed media of recent art school grads, performance art and special events like punk artist Braineater exhibitions that double as record promotions.

High-quality traditional art from Mainland China can be found at **C.C. Arts Centre** (20 East Pender). Further east in Japantown, **Everygreen Enterprises** (390 Powell) displays kimonos, pottery and printed rice paper. **Maro Gallery** (344) is the studio/showroom of ceramic artist Akiro Tomita.

North and South

Two public galleries that don't fit into these neighbourhoods but deserve a mention are **Presentation House** (333 Chesterfield, North Vancouver, 986-1351) which is the leading exhibitor of photography in B.C., and **Surrey Centennial Arts Centre** (13750 - 88th Ave., 596-7461) where you can see contemporary and historic exhibitions of leading local, national and international art. Both are about half an hour away from downtown Vancouver (don't attempt the drive in either direction after 4 p.m. when you'll be bumper to bumper with Surrey and North Vancouver commuters on their way home).

Historical Tour

Museums in Vancouver are different. It's not just that the historical subjects on display are different—as in places like the Grocery Hall of Fame or Pappas Fur Museum. The most striking difference is the physical setting and architecture of Vancouver's finest museums—features that will blow the spectacles off people who are accustomed to historical touring in other (less imaginative) cities.

For architecture, you couldn't hope for a more awe-inspiring structure to house the mystical relics of Northwest Coast Indians than Arthur Erickson's temple of cedar and glass—the Museum of Anthropology at U.B.C. For a natural setting, take the Centennial and Maritime Museums which sit side by side on Kits Point—Vanier Park in their backyard, English Bay in front.

Major League Museums

The largest civic collection in Canada is at the **Vancouver Centennial Museum** (1150 Chestnut, 736-7736) on the impeccably manicured spit of land that juts into English Bay between Kits Beach and Burrard Bridge. It constantly rotates its permanent collection, much to the disappointment of kids who always want to see the mummy. Main fixtures of the History Wing are life-sized replicas of part of an immigrant ship, a trading post, a CPR passenger car circa 1887 and rooms from Victorian and Edwardian homes reconstructed with siding and trim actually removed from the old homes before they were torn down.

A 10-minute walk west (aim for the towering totem pole) lands you at the **Maritime Museum** (1905 Ogden, 736-7736), home of the famous Royal Canadian Mounted Police patrol schooner *St. Roch.* The 60-year-old vessel, proclaimed a National Historic Site and displayed here in intricately restored splendour, was the first ship to sail both ways through the ice-bound Northwest Passage—quite a feat when you see how small the St. Roch is. Model ships and marine relics fill the main gallery while the mini-harbour welcomes visiting tall ships and other historic vessels from around the world.

There is a Pacific Northwest Coast Indian section in the Vancouver Museum, but if you want to see the very best collection of its kind displayed in perfectly compatible surroundings, head to U.B.C.'s **Museum of Anthropology** (228-5087). The award-winning Arthur Erickson-designed building housing the Indian art and artifacts includes one room that makes you feel ant-sized—the Great Hall filled with massive totem poles. The museum perches on the forested Point Grey cliffs, its 14-metre-high windows looking out across English Bay to the north. In the museum's own backyard is a reconstructed Indian village with Haida dwellings and contemporary totem poles visible from the Great Hall.

Offbeat Treasures

If you want to put a sweet perspective on Vancouver's history, visit the **B.C. Sugar Museum** (foot of Rogers St., 253-1131) at the Port of Vancouver. This little museum is contained within the B.C. Sugar Refinery, historically and currently one of Vancouver's biggest businesses. Founded by B.T. Rogers in 1891, the sugar refinery's growth roughly parallels the development of the port city, a theme that is played up in the displays of photographs and equipment. A 25-minute film is shown at frequent intervals, and tours are offered for groups of eight to 30 people.

Thousands of people stroll Jericho Beach year round, but how many have even noticed the **Old Hastings Mill Store** (1575 Alma St., 228-1213) tucked away behind the Royal Vancouver Yacht Club? When I paid my respects to Vancouver's first general store, it was just me and the teetering shelves full of wooden nails and sewing baskets and moustache cups. If you get the sense that this relic of the old port town doesn't belong here, it's because it really doesn't. The shiplap-sided store was floated here by barge from its original location at (where else?) the Hastings Mill which has since been cleared away in the name of Burrard Inlet port expansion. The store is a browser's gold mine, but unfortunately its hours are as irregular as its stock.

The Grocery Hall of Fame (1241 Homer St., 669-2214) is something of an overstatement. This quirky little storefront museum is strictly for food nostalgia buffs who haven't forgiven Campbell's for canning the kids on their label, and can't stand tea that comes in cardboard rather than tin. For food futurists, there is also a section on groceries in the year 2010. Good for a lark, mornings only.

Here's a free museum that might well end up being extremely expensive. **Pappas Furs** (449 Hamilton St., 681-6391) maintains an active trading post in the shop, offering visitors a view of the historic barter system that launched this family business in the early part of the century. Constantine Pappas and his staff allow you to buy or barter for Native B.C. crafts on display in the shop, and are only too happy to illustrate the fur business by dipping into their stock of exquisite new furs.

Worth the Drive

These museums are far flung, but if you have special interests in steam trains, trading posts or copper mining, you might not mind the hour or so behind the wheel. They are especially suited to kids, so if you have some of those restless critters on hand for the afternoon you can easily turn the distance factor into a plus. Just bring ice cream money and a bucketful of back-seat games.

Heritage Village Museum (4900 Deer Lake Ave., 294-1233) in Burnaby's Century Park takes the prize for combining authenticity with good old-fashioned fun. It's particularly delightful here on holidays when the staff dresses up in turn-of-the century costumes and brings the "village" to life—blacksmith shop, antique printing press, dentist's office, Royal Bank, Chinese herbalist, school house and all kinds of other display buildings. There are regular demonstrations of Andy Anderson's original steam-powered sawmill from Powell River, and a rail car from B.C. Electric's 1913 "Interurban Tram" that served Burnaby for half a century. A miniature steam train offers rides around the outskirts of the village, but if it's raining too hard you can always bob in to the Bob Inn (excuse me) for a snack. This place is seriously cute (don't say I didn't warn you). Guided 90-minute tours are the best way to see the works, offered twice a day in spring and summer.

The B.C. Museum of Mining (toll free phone: 688-8735) is not at all cute if you suffer claustrophobia, but if you don't mind tunneling deep into a mountainside in adapted carts you'll find it any eye-opening experience. The 75-year-old copper mine at Britannia Beach on Hwy. 99 (52 km. north of Vancouver) has been converted into a virtual mountain of working displays. Tours include the giant concentrator building which at its peak processed more copper than any other in the British Empire and Lost Creek where you can try your hand at gold panning. The Cook Tent provides refreshments and a gift shop full of mining mementos. Open May 9 through Labour Day.

If you want to go right back to the beginning of white settlement in B.C., a visit to **Fort Langley National Historic Park** (48 km. east on Hwy. 1, 888-4424) will tell you the whole story in one neat lesson. Hudson's Bay Company built the fort settlement in 1827, before there was a Vancouver or Victoria, to secure the Fraser River as a trading route. Besides giving birth to the region's fur trade, this park is also the site of the first salmon-packing operation and the first wheat grown for export. It's all well displayed—the palisades, main gates, officers' quarters, artisans' shops and original company store (lots of shelter). Regular guided tours, year round.

Reading Tour

If you simply want to pick up a good paperback thriller to take to your armchair for a warm, dry day of escape, drop into any of the major department-store book sections, or one of the large chains (**W.H. Smith** in Vancouver Centre and a number of outlying malls, **Classic Bookshop** and **Coles** in Pacific Centre) and you will certainly find what you need.

But if you are a connoisseur—if you want the latest

hard-cover edition of your favourite German author in translation, or a text on advanced photographic technique, or some rare antiquarian treasure—let's spend the afternoon together. Browsing, comparison shopping and chatting with the bespectacled young lady behind the counter is as important a part of your reading tour as buying the book. On rainy days, especially, there is no point hurrying through your book-shopping list.

First, a few words about the **Vancouver Public Library.** Can't complain about the folks who work there (friendly, helpful) or the service (surprisingly efficient for such a monster institution) but the Main Branch Building (750 Robson, 665-2280) won't win any awards for comfort. Perhaps they're afraid that if they put one cushioned armchair in the reading room, the entire transient population of Vancouver would camp out on it. Perhaps they're right. In any case, this 30-year-old bare box of a building is a great place for checking out books, catching up on the daily news in Budapest or Manila, or finding out the Queen Mom's middle name. But if you want to linger, head for one of the newer branches.

The renovated **Oakridge** branch (Oakridge Shopping Centre, 261-1516) is bright, cheerful and comfortable; **Riley Park** (3981 Main, 872-0844) and **Mount Pleasant** (370 East Broadway, 872-1331) are good family-oriented facilities with "story pits" where kids can curl up and read; and the **Joe Fortes** branch at the West End Community Centre (870 Denman, 682-8024) is a pretty good lounging library with windows offering lively Denman Street views.

New Books

There is only one place to start your tour: **Duthie Books,** headquartered at 919 Robson (684-4496) with smaller branches at Arbutus Village (738-1833) and at 4444 West 10th near U.B.C. (224-7012). Duthie's has the kind of selection, particularly in the hard-cover section of the Robson store, that no other store could afford to stock. You can find something like 20,000 books on the main floor, including extensive fiction, biography and history sections. The best travel section in the city is here, plus the most diverse and expensive stock of art, architecture and photography books. There is a well-stocked children's corner, and a broad selection in the Paperback Cellar down the spiral staircase.

Celia Duthie runs the stores now that her father Bill has retired, and the little empire has grown since she took the helm. Recently she has opened **Manhattan Books**

(1019 Robson, 681-9074) which stocks a good, general selection of remaindered books, strongest in fiction, biography and art. There is also a tasteful selection of fashion and special-interest magazines. Through the courtyard of the beautifully renovated Manhattan Apartments (a Vancouver landmark) is the new **M.C. Duthie Gallery** and beside it **Binky's Oyster Bar & Restaurant** (see Lunch: Posh, page 115). Celia also publishes *The Reader,* a periodical available free at the better bookstores, containing reviews of current releases.

Blackberry Books offers a smaller but well balanced selection in a bright, white environment some people prefer to the vast scale of Duthie's. Staff is very helpful and informed; there is usually soft classical music in the background. Owner Lucy Stewart, whose knowledge is seasoned by 20 years in the trade, is usually on hand at the Granville Island shop (1663 Duranleau, 685-4113) where the specialties are wine books, cooking, art and architecture. Stock at the newer Kitsilano store (2206 West 4th, 733-1673) leans toward literature in paperback.

Two other small, dependable shops are **Hager Books**

(2176 West 41st, 293-9412) which has a fairly conservative selection of current hard and soft covers to reflect its Kerrisdale clientele, and **English Bay Book Co.** (1184 Denman, 688-6344) which does a fine job servicing the West End's more cosmopolitan tastes.

Vancouver's supermarket of books is at **U.B.C.** (228-4741 for directions into the campus) where a recent $7 million enlargement made room for some 30,000 titles as well as a computer section, stationery department and gift shop where you can buy everything down to a piggy bank with the U.B.C. insignia emblazoned on it. Of course most of the stock is texts, but you'll also find a good variety of fiction (especially Canadian) in the Leisure Reading section, plus the best variety in the city of foreign language books. It will order virtually any book from any country, and getting service is no problem with 65 full-time staff on hand plus 25 student part-timers.

And for bargains, stop by Sharman King's **Book Warehouse** (632 West Broadway) where you'll find the largest selection of remaindered books in the city, plus a variety of new releases and best sellers at discounted prices.

Secondhand Books

One name springs to the lips of collectors and connoisseurs—**William Hoffer, Bookseller** (58 Powell, 683-3022). Hoffer, who can be a tease at best and a terrible snob at worst, has been in a few different locations before settling into this atmospheric Gastown shop. Despite his rough edge, he has a faithful clientele that keeps following him wherever he goes. He runs one of Canada's most distinguished antiquarian and secondhand bookstores, specializing in Canadian literature. If you are looking for rare treasures, ask Hoffer to take you into the back room. Just one word of warning: Don't even think about bargaining. (That goes for all the antiquarian book stores.) If a hardcover is marked $8, you are already getting a bargain. If it's $30, that is what the dealer's catalogue lists it at. You're not at a flea market here.

There are a lot of poets and writers in the city who credit Don Stewart of **MacLeod's Books** (455 West Pender, 681-7654) with holding the literary/political community together almost single-handedly. MacLeod's selection ranges broadly across literature, history, art and Canadiana, but Stewart can be counted on to stock additional items you won't find anywhere else—books from the FBI's library on radicalism, 1950s nostalgia paperbacks, antiquarian books in the humanities, and other backroom treasures. Stewart's radical leanings can be gleaned from newspapers, leaflets and posters that crowd his desk area. Want to find out what you can do to protest American involvement in Latin America? Look here. There's also a children's book corner, thoughtfully fitted with mini-table, chairs and toys.

This section of Pender has been dubbed "book alley" by local history buff and journalist Chuck Davis. **Terry Rutherford Bookseller** (420 West Pender, 682-8227) specializes in mystery and detective novels but there is also a large section of science fiction. **A.J. Ainsworth Books** (321 West Pender, 682-2015) feels more like owner Doreen Crombie's cozy living room than a store. It's crammed floor to ceiling with old and very old books, many going back to the day Doreen's father A.J. opened shop here in 1939. She has been holding the fort for the last 30 years. **McIntyre's** (319 West Pender, 684-8611), upstairs from Ainsworth's, specializes in books on ships, the sea and railways. (For aviation books, your best bet is **Bomber Joe's,** a bizarre little place run by pilot Riley Burke in the old Airport South building—head for Vancouver International Airport and watch for the turn-off about a mile before you get to the big terminal.)

Back on book alley, **Bond's** (532 Richards, 688-5227) has an impressive antiquarian and illustrated book collection, especially in Canadian and Northern history, travel and art. Swinging south toward Gastown you come to the literary **Colophon Books** (407 West Cordova, 685-4138) displaying special editions including Black Sparrow Press poetry.

Noteworthy for its broad general selection and hard-to-get social/literary magazines is **Octopus Books** at two locations (2250 West 4th, 732-8721 and 1146 Commercial, 253-0913).

Specialty Books

On "book alley" the best selection of cookbooks is **Chef Bell's** (669-2910), tucked away in an upstairs nook at 335 West Pender. Someone told me there are 2,000 cookbooks crammed into this room, but who's counting? Once you've met and chatted with 75-year-old Lionel Bell the figures lose significance. He's a charming and incredibly knowledgeable old chef who always slips a few good recipes to the people he likes.

If you want to get a book and get centred at the same time, **Banyen Books** (2685 West Broadway, 732-7912) is the place. There is an impeccably organized selection of psychology, holistic health, esoteric philosophy and "consciousness" books here, suitably enriched by a stay-awhile-and-relax atmosphere. The air is heavy with incense, classical (often Eastern) music plays softly and you can rest your bones on cushioned benches tucked among the shelves.

West 4th is the street for women and children. **Ariel** (2766 West 4th, 733-3511) has feminist theory, lesbian and gay studies, assertiveness, birth books and some Canadiana. **Peregrine** (2950 West 4th, 738-6523) is slightly softer core with women's studies, psychology, childcare and a small but nicely chosen selection of children's books.

One of my favourite Saturday afternoon haunts when I have little Abby in tow, **Vancouver Kidsbooks** (2868 West 4th, 738-5335), has not only the best kids' selection in town but the best means of distraction while mom is making her choice (see page 76).

For kids young and old, **The Comicshop** (2089 West 4th, 738-8122) has the largest new and used comic collection in the country, plus science fiction, fanzines, posters and prints. Specializing in science fiction, **White Dwarf Books** (4374 West 10th, 228-8223) and **Mall Book Bazaar** (850 Granville, 687-2213) carry all the top authors plus collections.

Religious bookshops of note are **The Anglican Bookshop** (167 West Pender, 681-2625), **Christian Supplies** (501 Dunsmuir, 681-9335), **Shalom Books & Gifts** (3712 Oak, 734-1106) for Jewish subjects and **Fraser Book Nook** (6219 Fraser, 325-7118) which carries Bibles in 30 languages.

Sophia Bookstore (725 Nelson, 684-4032) specializes in Japan and the Far East. **Le Bouquineur** (1222 Robson, 687-5936) has mostly French books, a few German, plus lots of instructional material.

If your tastes lean to the political left, you will probably find what you need at **People's Co-op Bookstore** (1391 Commercial, 253-6442). Canadian and B.C. government acts, statistics, maps and a wide variety of official literature from international agencies can be found at **Renouf Books & Maps** (522 West Hastings, 687-3320).

And finally, books for music lovers: Vancouver does not have a music book specialist but the main **Duthie Books** store (919 Robson, 684-4496) has a decent section on music, chiefly classical. You can take out books as well as musical scores from the **Vancouver Public Library** (see page 52) or the **Canadian Music Centre** (#3 - 2007 West 4th, 734-4622) which runs a free lending library of some 6,500 scores by Canadian composers, plus catalogues, recordings and educational resources of all kinds. For new wave music buffs, **Odyssey Imports** (866 Granville, 669-6644) carries the most up-to-date rock books as well as imported records and band memorabilia.

Notes on News

European News & Imports (1136 Robson, 683-0616) is the old-time favourite newsstand offering an eclectic jumble of magazines, newspapers, paperbacks, glassware, nicknacks and, of all things, a Dirndl Boutique. We're in the heart of Robsonstrasse, which explains the dirndls and the oom-pa-pa polkas that are amplified through the store and out onto the street. The place is cluttered, busy and noisy, but if you persevere you'll soon discover the printed matter is actually quite well organized into Canadian and foreign dailies, news magazines, women's and fashion magazines, technology, ski and outdoors, muscles mags and a huge (one might say grotesque) porn section. It is open until 10 p.m. daily.

European's chief contender is **International** in the basement of Gastown's Le Magasin, 332 Water St., 685-8141. By comparison, International is quiet, spacious, high-tech in decor and sophisticated in selection. Magazines are displayed on the wall like art, and some of the prices lend justification. The best selection of city magazines from across the continent is here, plus plenty of high-gloss fashion and glamour. Open daily to 6 p.m., Sunday to 5.

The best newspaper books section is in the *Vancouver Sun* on Saturdays. Shorter and a little less distinguished is the review section in the Magazine section of *The Sunday Province*.

Stage & Screen

Entertainment sections in the Friday newspapers, either *The Sun* or *The Province*, tell you much more about what's happening on stage and screen than I possibly can in this section. I also like the listing in the weekly *Westender's* "What's On" section, and the monthly "In Town" section of *Vancouver Magazine*. Only problem with the news media is it tells you everything about what's on but not very much about what's good. That's where I come in. Below, a dangerously generalized, certainly biased guide to your best bets in Vancouver's performing arts and cinema:

Theatre

The regional company that receives most of the government grant money is the **Vancouver Playhouse** (872-6622), often slammed by the critics for not living up to its mandate but generally loved by the public for being so darned sophisticated about whatever it does. No other company can afford such fine costumes and elaborate sets, nor such acclaimed Eastern Canadian stars to stud its cast lists. Its mainstage "Red Series" at the **Queen Elizabeth Playhouse** (649 Cambie) leans toward the European and modern American classics plus some safe contemporary Canadiana. The alternate "Blue Series" features more risky material, including original Vancouver scripts. Vancouver East Cultural Centre (below) hosts the Blue Series in its intimate 280-seat theatre.

The **Arts Club** started out 20 years ago as a nervy little alternate theatre, but today it is a multi-facility empire with a subscription list rivalling any in Western Canada. Director Bill Millerd is the restless spirit behind this fast-growing company, shrewdly pushing onto new frontiers to prevent the art from turning crusty or conservative with size. His mainstage on **Granville Island** (1585 Johnston, 687-1644) plays it fairly straight with sure-fire-hit material including musical comedies and American pop classics. More risky material is presented at the original **Arts Club Theatre** at 1181 Seymour St., and cabaret-style entertainment washes down with full bar service at the new **Arts Club Revue Theatre** next door to the big Granville Island stage.

The **Vancouver East Cultural Centre** (1895 Venables, 254-9578) has been popular with young, artsy types ever since they were hippies. The same crowd that used to pour in from Kitsilano and Point Grey in search of light politics and heavy cheesecake now struts in for sophisticated comedy, fringe theatre and (see below) fine classical music. Besides the popular Playhouse Blue Series, VECC plays host to some of the hottest new touring productions in the country, plus the local works of the politically conscious **Tamahnous Theatre** which can take credit for developing some of the most important new plays to emerge from Vancouver in the past decade. I like this place a lot, not only for the off-beat productions but for the folksy atmosphere of this converted church and the friendly people who run it.

The **New Play Centre** (685-6228) is one of those creatively important institutions that misses at least as often as it hits. If you want to get into the creative stream, watch out for script development workshops, readings, final productions and new play festivals staged at the cramped but colourful Waterfront Theatre on Granville Island (1512 Anderson).

For just plain good (bordering on zany) times, check out the **Theatresports** schedule at **City Stage** (751 Thurlow, 688-7013). This improvisational play-off has become one of the city's most popular late-night arts attractions in the past few years. There is more chutzpa here than talent, judges rather than critics, and the audience gets more into cat-calls than applause. A rowdy time is guaranteed. Generally weekends only. A more sensible crowd gathers at City Stage daily at noon for lunchtime theatre, featuring lightweight but often very entertaining one-act plays.

Movies

As the cinemas in the downtown core and the suburban malls divide and subdivide into theatre complexes like Capital 6 and Cineplex, it's nice to know that deep in the residential neighbourhoods there still exist old-style movie houses where you can chat with the house manager about the coming attractions and you can get coffee to drink and popcorn with real butter. If those things matter to you, keep an eye out for what's showing at cinemas like **The Park,** 3440 Cambie, **The Stanley,** 2750 Granville, **The Varsity,** 4375 West 10th (home of the Vancouver International Film Festival), **The Bay,** 935 Denman, **The Dunbar,** 4555 Dunbar, and **The Ridge,** 3131 Arbutus. They're all old but not old-fashioned cinemas, having properly updated their sound systems and touched up their fake rococo/deco/romanesque decor. The old seats are not always as comfortable, but I find that such minor inconveniences dissolve when I'm sipping peppermint tea (The Bay) or munching nanaimo bars (The Varsity).

Program choices are often better at the older cinemas than at the fancy new ones. **The Ridge** is the foremost example. Owner Leonard Schein has turned this sleepy neighbourhood movie house into a mecca for serious film buffs and rerun addicts. I don't know how he gets his hands on so many brand new uncut prints of old classics, first releases of Cannes award winners or sensational rock movies, but one way or another you can trust Schein to pack at least a dozen great flicks into each month's schedule. On top of that, every Sunday features the children's matinees at 2 p.m. (see page 74) and the CFOX rock movie series at 4:30 p.m. Ridge regulars don't even try to remember what's coming; they pick up the broadsheet program notes whenever they go, and paste them religiously on the fridge at home. You can get info or be put on the mailing list by calling 738-6311.

If you like what's happening at The Ridge, check out Schein's second rerun theatre, **Vancouver East Cinema** (2290 Commercial) which has a similarly eclectic program with a more popular edge. Call for a program sheet, 253-5455.

For devotees of the serious art of film, regular Ridge visits should be supplemented by the odd evening at **Pacific Cinematheque** (1616 West 3rd, 732-6119) which is more of a clubhouse than a movie house. The cream of the local film-making community gathers here to show their work to one another and (to a lesser degree) the public. They also show some acclaimed international and cult films, plus excellent series which draw so well that they often screen them at the larger Robson Square Media Centre's theatre (800 Hornby St.). Programs available free at **Duthie Books** (919 Robson) or **Vancouver Public Library.**

Classical Notes

Two good reasons to go to a concert by the **Vancouver Symphony Orchestra** (875-1661): it's a first-rate orchestra, and it performs in the exquisite monument to vaudeville theatre, **The Orpheum** (884 Granville). Built in 1926 as a western outpost of the Chicago-based orpheum vaudeville circuit, the 2,800-seat, multi-levelled theatre is as rich in acoustics as it is in decor—marble/travertine walls, Spanish arches, incredible plasterwork ceiling and all. In 1973 a much drearier version of the revitalized Orpheum, then used as a movie house, came a hair's breadth from conversion into a Famous Players cinemaplex. A grass-roots "Save the Orpheum" movement won the day, convincing the city to buy and lavishly renovate the theatre. A new lobby was added in 1983 after years of patrons' complaints that they couldn't squeeze into the washrooms at intermission. In all, it's a place worth seeing no matter what you hear while you're there.

Conductor Kazuyoshi Akiyama and the orchestra present an amazing variety of series and recitals throughout the year, including the **Great Composers** series for classics lovers, **Seagram Pops** if your taste runs to "Andre Gagnon Goes Gold" or "Mancini Mania" and **Sun Family Pops** starring the likes of Big Bird.

The Orpheum's modern counterpart is the **Queen Elizabeth Theatre** (630 Hamilton). It is architecturally plain though functional by comparison. **Vancouver Opera Association** (682-2871) puts on its lavishly produced shows here four times a year. A hard-core opera following has grown with the VOA since its birth 25 years ago, and a cry has gone up for more than the four productions. One solution offered by the **Vancouver Opera Club** (681-1886) is to organize regular bus excursions to the **Seattle Opera House,** leaving the Saturday morning of each show and returning that night after curtain.

There's nothing like chamber music to warm the soul on rainy days—especially rainy Sundays. There are **Sunday Coffee Concerts** (736-7661) at 11 a.m. September through May at the Queen Elizabeth Theatre, featuring family-oriented concerts of classical and modern music, dance and mime. And here's a treat: it offers babysitting, $1.50 for the hour-long concert. And at the intimate Vancouver East Cultural Centre, **Masterpiece Music** (254-9578) presents a series of ten Sunday afternoon and evening concerts through the year. At the

Bosendorfer concert grand is pianist Linda Lee Thomas, artistic director of the dynamic Masterpiece Trio who perform a mixed but relatively safe program along with different guest artists each time.

Vancouver is also a hot choir town, boasting two of Canada's leading ensembles: Jon Washburn's **Vancouver Chamber Choir** (738-6822) for the choral connoisseurs, performing a varied season at The Orpheum as well as Ryerson United Church and **Vancouver Bach Choir** (921-8012) which presents a knock-out Sing-Along Messiah each Christmas as well as regular concerts at The Orpheum.

On the little stage, things are looking up for dance. Vancouver has given birth to some very exciting but rather under-exposed contemporary dance companies, notably the **Anna Wyman Dance Theatre, Terminal Dance** and **Paula Ross Dancers.** No regular seasons, so watch the papers for dates.

Buying classical: **The Magic Flute** (2100 West 4th, 736-2727) and **Sikora's Classical Records** (432 West Hastings, 685-0625) both claim to have the largest selection in Western Canada. I haven't counted, but at a glance I'd say they both win. Both also have very helpful and informed staff.

Playing classical: Whether you want sheet music, instruments or instrument repair, **Ward Music** (412 West Hastings, 682-5288) is the shop of repute. If you don't see what you want, ask. They'll find it or order it.

GOT KIDS

Playing With

Let me come clean: I've been using Dan Wood's excellent *Kids! Kids! Kids!* book for myself for years now, and none of the grown-ups I've dragged around with me have complained. There is so much happening in this city for the young and young at heart that you'll find a number of guidebooks devoted to them, notably Dan's (look for the 1984 edition) and the annual *Kids' Guide to Vancouver* by Janet Lee and Rae Schidlo. The Kid's Guide is rather awkwardly set up in a calendar format but has a handy index for quick referral. Both guides are available at major bookstores.

But be honest with yourself. Do you want to play with your kids today or would you rather get somebody else to do the honours so you can go out and play? If you want a sitter to come to your home or hotel, Anne Garber's semi-annual *Babysitter Directory* (call 263-8081 for details) lists qualified teenage sitters by area.

If you prefer group daycare, you can't get any better than the YWCA's emergency and short-term daycare center, **Granny Y's,** at 1140 West Pender (new phone). They try to accommodate youngsters under five at short notice in an emergency, but usually require three or four days notice to fit your child into their busy schedule. The fee in 1984 is $3 an hour. I can personally vouch for Granny Y's; my daughter Abby has been there dozens of times and she always comes home happy.

Babies & Tots

Community centres are by far the best resource in the city for parents and tots. There are 25 different centres in Metro Vancouver, each offering a variety of drop-in and member play programs. (Visitors are welcome to attend any of the drop-in programs.) Your best bet is to check the Yellow Pages listing under Recreation Centres for the place nearest you and ask for their schedules. I can personally vouch for the **Gymn and Sing** class every Friday morning at Kerrisdale Community Centre where the under-three set (escorted by parents) take their first tumbles on trampolines, balance boards, slides and ring-swings. Almost every centre has its own version of this program, usually charging about $1.50.

Waterbabies is another popular activity at the community centres that have pools. Probably the best pool for little splashers is at the **Vancouver Aquatic**

Centre (1050 Beach, 689-7156), where there is a specially designed paddling-and-learning pool beside the big one. Moms and tots pack the place Monday, Wednesday and Friday mornings when the Aquatic Centre offers babysitting—$1 per child, 9:30-11:30 a.m. Mom can have her swim and sauna, or take a fitness class, then take baby in for a splash. In east-end Vancouver, **Kensington Pool** (5175 Dumfries, 327-9401) has a similar arrangement, and an ideal learning pool for tiny ones.

Family Place can be a lifesaver on those interminable rainy afternoons at home or in your cramped hotel room. The kids are fingerpainting the walls and you're climbing them. Why not pack them into the car and head for one of the half-dozen Family Place drop-in centres where they can paint somebody else's walls? These are supervised playrooms filled with used toys and jungle-gymns, drawing easels and bookshelves. Parents are expected to keep an eye on their kids most of the time, but they can ask a staff member to cover for them now and then so they can sit down with a coffee and a magazine in the adjoining lounge. Drop-in fee is 50¢. Call 731-2719 or 255-9841 for the Family Place nearest you.

Bigger Kids

If your kids are like the ones I know, as soon as they're old enough to put on a raincoat, all they want to do is go out in it. If you have a back alley or neighbourhood park, you don't need my ideas on rainy-day entertainment. Nothing I can suggest comes close to the fun they'll have with their own puddle-jumping, dam-building and matchbox-sailing ingenuity. Only problem is, you may find yourself excluded. So if you're looking for a family outing, let me suggest a few destinations that will provide at least intermittent shelter and plenty of stimulation for the little ones and big ones in your party:

Granville Island answers every parent's rainy-day dilemma. There are more neat things to do on this tiny piece of land under the Granville Bridge than in the entire downtown core. Start with the **Public Market** (you can't miss it, just head west) where kids will be mesmerized by Atilio the singing pasta maker, Mario's spaghetti-shaped ice cream, the fudge maker stooped over his chocolate-covered slab of marble, the giant donut machine and (on weekends) Dan the One-Man Band who plays/sings/strums/bangs/stomps/clangs away on his incredible music-mobile just outside the main entrance.

Other attractions around Granville Island: Visit the **Lobster Man** (1604 Duranleau, 687-4228) where you are surrounded by enormous tanks of live creepers flown in from the East Coast. These folks supply lobster and other shellfish to the best restaurants in town, but they'll sell it to you at a much better price right out of the tank. If you prefer to see the non-creeping wonders of the sea, stop by **The Ocean Floor** (1520 Duranleau, 681-5014) and check out the display of coral, shells and what-not.

If it's summer, let the kids loose in the sheltered **Adventure Playground** next to False Creek Community Centre (1318 Cartwright, 688-9478). It's a safe construction site for mini-builders—all the materials supplied.

And for the little literary set, one of the city's best bookstores is on the island—**Blackberry Books** (1663 Duranleau, 685-4113) with a well stocked kiddies' reading corner. If you're looking for a lunch spot to complete your tour, see Eating with Kids on page 71.

Granville Island's one drawback is the weekend congestion, so here are a couple of alternatives: **Chinatown** (page 19) and **Gastown** (page 27) are filled with colourful shops, off-beat tourist attractions and snack stops. In Chinatown, don't miss the herbalists, the barbequed meat shops and jam-packed trading companies where you can buy toys and trinkets that are really cheap and really different.

In Gastown there are shops wholly dedicated to kites **(High as a Kite,** 131 Water St., 687-8041) and dolls **(Doll's House,** right next door, 687-3655) and all kinds of glorified junk. And no matter what Mom and Dad think, kids go crazy over the **Gastown Wax Museum** (1 Alexander, 685-2751) which is a genuine imitation of Madame Tussaud's with everything from Churchill to James Dean, The Last Supper to The Chamber of Horrors. Aghhhh!

Kids aren't the only creatures that don't mind getting wet—animals, on the whole, don't seem to mind either. Putting two and two together, you realize rainy days are actually ideal times to visit the zoo, provided you are dressed for it. You and your kids will be able to commune quietly and personally with the animals in the absence of the usual crowds, and you won't have to wait in line for your hotdogs.

Different strokes for different folks, but my choice is the petting zoo at **Stanley Park** (681-8729) where little kids can cuddle right up to little kids. It is a five minute walk to the "big" zoo (681-1141) where you had best keep your distance from the bears, monkeys, seals, penguins and reptiles. The big zoo is open year round, but the petting zoo is open daily May to September, and on weekends only during the cold months. Both are free. Shelter is limited at the Stanley Park zoos, but if you want to dry off and see some incredible marine animals, you are not far from the Public Aquarium (details on page 90).

A wild and, no doubt, wet experience is ensured at the **Richmond Nature Park** (1185 Westminster Hwy., 273-7015) where you can stroll the boardwalk alongside wild rabbits, all kinds of waterfowl and the odd fox. You can get out of the rain into the Nature House where live and preserved critters are very impressively displayed. It's all free, including nature films on Sundays, 1 to 4 p.m.

From November through March rain in the city usually means snow in the mountains, so if you have an adventuring spirit, go for it! There is good tobogganing and cross-country skiing at **Cypress Bowl** in West Vancouver, about 15 minutes by car from downtown (call 926-8644 for directions, or to book bus tickets on weekends only).

The whole family can safely ski Cypress or **Grouse**

Mountain (324-3211) thanks to the excellent **Anklebiters** and **Ski-Wee** programs for pre-schoolers. Of course excellence has a price. Both mountains charge $10 a lesson, $15 if you have to rent equipment. There is no public transit to Cypress, only a private charter on weekends which doesn't fit the Anklebiters schedule. But Grouse is serviced daily by Metro Transit.

Big Kids

If your preteeners and adolescents are still open to suggestion, count yourself lucky. Most of the kids over 10 that I know are perfectly happy left to their own devices, but that doesn't mean their parents are perfectly happy dropping them off at McDonald's for the entire afternoon. Here are a few alternatives worth a try:

All the community centres have open gymns scheduled at various times for basketball practise, open rinks for drop-in hockey and pools for kids-only swimming so that adult length-swimmers won't impede their horseplay. Some centres host clubs dedicated to Dungeons and Dragons, computer programming and assorted esoterica. Because these centres change their schedules seasonally, call for an activities list. You'll find all of them listed under **Recreation Centres** in the Yellow Pages, and if you are unfamiliar with the city you can choose the one nearest you by matching the first two digits of your phone number with the centre numbers listed. Most of the centres (including pools and rinks) are operated by the Vancouver **Park Board** (681-1141) which can also be helpful in locating the activity you want. For more detail on pools and rinks, see Reclamation and Recreation, page 80.

By the time kids get to this age, it is impossible to speak of them as a group. They are as like one another as I am like the bank manager who lives next door. If your child is brainy, the **Arts, Sciences and Technology Centre** will occupy him for days (see Kid Culture, page 75); if she is artsy, **Vancouver Art Gallery's** special room for kids (page 75) will act as a primer for an extended tour of the whole magnificent building; if she's sporty, the **B.C. Place Stadium** tour might be an idea (see Spectator Sports, page 82); if he's into quirky old stuff, check out the museums in Historical Tour (page 48); and the parents of a blooming nature buff will find plenty of suggestions in Nature Under Cover (page 90).

On The Town With

Want to know why some parents can go out for a whole day with their kids, get all their shopping done, have a nice dinner out and come home tired but happy while others get home with nothing accomplished and egg (literally) all over their faces? The difference is, some parents know where to go.

Shopping With

If you have serious shopping to do, your best plan is to head for the suburban malls. At both **Coquitlam Centre** (2929 Barnet Hwy., 464-3141) and **Guildford Town Centre** (104 Ave. and 152 St. in Surrey, 588-5454) there are **Paddington Station Child Minding Centres** where government-licensed staff will entertain, feed, change and cuddle your pre-schooler while you do your shopping. These are excellent facilities with responsible child-staff ratios and safe, clean furnishings. You pay $2 an hour per child, less if you have your Paddington ticket validated at any number of the mall stores. Call ahead to reserve space.

Unfortunately the downtown malls are not nearly so well equipped for children, especially those in strollers. At the large **Pacific Centre** (700 W. Georgia) elevators are inconveniently situated for access to a number of the shops, which leads many to take the perilous trip up escalators with tots in strollers. Watch out! The sprawling **Park Royal Mall** in West Vancouver (Marine at Taylor Way) is better, with features like a carpeted play pit and a moving sidewalk.

Of the large department stores, **Woodward's** (in eight locations) tops the list for childmindedness. Their mothers' rooms are equipped with cots, change tables and arm chairs, their dining rooms have children's menus and carts in their grocery departments come with safety belts (ask at the service desk if you don't see them). **Eaton's** isn't far behind, and moving up fast.

A lot of stores have gimmicks to attract kids—like the Cookie Credit Card at **Safeway** that entitles the bearer to a free cookie with every visit, and the Better Birthday Club at **The Bay** which offers members a free hamburger lunch.

But the most elaborate kiddie bait is strung by **Ikea,** the "impossible" Swedish furniture-and-more store in Richmond (3200 Sweden Way, 273-2051). This enormous, new flagship store for North American Ikea has an awful lot of kids believing it's actually a playground just for them. There is a supervised "ballroom" in which kids aged three to seven can slide into a foot-deep cushion of plastic balls; kids eight to 12 have their own "creative room" where they can draw, colour or listen to stories and rock music through headphones. The under-three set get free strollers and even (get this!) free diapers—there is a spacious, beautifully furnished and stocked changing room. And all kids like Ikea's cafeteria where they can order from their own menu and sit at tables their own size. (Even the toilets here are nice and low.)

Shopping For

I have surveyed all the new-age parents I know to come up with this short list of clothing and toy shops that fit the same criteria as above. You will find most everything you need in them, and your kids will be pleasantly diverted from such common pursuits as dragging everything from the shelves onto the floor.

For toys, **Kinderspel** (3039 Granville, 734-0321) has the most sophisticated selection in town, including European brands like Ambi and Brio, beautiful Korean dolls and the best of the North American manufacturers. You won't find a single Smurf or CareBear in the place. The fine toys are high enough up that your toddler can't grab them, but there are lots of attractive, clunky things low down to keep him busy while you scout around. Take your older child downstairs to do some hands-on exploration of computer and electronic games. A note of caution: bring lots of money.

There is more variety at more moderate prices in the long-established Kerrisdale shop, **Windmill Toys** (2387 -West 41st, 261-2120). You'll find quality educational toys as well as commercial stuff right up to the rafters, and if you forget what you came in for you're bound to leave with something else that you like just as well. There is a room at the back with giant stuffed animals, mini-furniture and a toy train half-way up the wall going round and round that will drive you crazy but keep the kids happy for at least 20 minutes.

The very best deals on toys are at **The Toy Exchange,** a consignment/secondhand store in two locations—North Vancouver (141 East 2nd, 985-TOYS) and Steveston (3480B Moncton, 272-4447). Take back that SuperSwing Katie never sits in and trade it for the Fisher-Price garage. There's big stuff, little stuff, wrecked stuff and nice stuff. Be prepared to dig around.

You'll find hand-made toys as well as other artsy-crafts

at the **Burnaby Arts Centre** (Century Park, 6450 Gilpin, 298-7322) which holds crafts markets on the first and third Sunday of each month, 11 a.m. to 4 p.m. If you're worried about your wild ones breaking teapots and unravelling macrame, send them upstairs to the Creative Play Centre where supervisor Marian Rutter will keep an eye on them while you browse. (No charge.)

The nicest arrangement I've seen for restless kids in a clothing store is at **Kiddly Winks** (3385 West 4th, 733-6546) where designer/owner Peggy Warren has a well-organized play table tucked in a quiet corner. This is a tiny shop with rarely more than two customers at a time, which means you get all of Peggy's personal attention and your kid gets all the toys. The appliqued overalls and jumpers she makes are adorable and not too pricey. She carries a few quality lines of tops and cotton underwear as well.

Kiss a Rhino (3095 West Broadway, 734-0953) has a good variety of quality children's lines including some, like the rainbow-coloured "Wibbies" T-shirts and underwear from New England, that you won't see anywhere else. There is a large playroom with resident six-foot teddybear, and a proper mother's room.

Other favourites are **Peppermintree** (4243 Dunbar, 228-9815) which has one of the largest and finest stocks in the popular price range; **Czar Nicholas and the Toad** (2375 West 41st, 263-9313) which adjoins Windmill Toys and caters to the pre- and Private School crowd; and **Bratz** (2828 Granville, 734-4344) for infants to teens who wouldn't be caught dead in anything less expensive than Norma Kamali.

Eating With

If you followed my main piece of advice about touring Granville Island with kids (page 66) finish up with a meal at **Isadora's** (1540 Old Bridge St., Granville Island, 681-3748). This is the only child-oriented restaurant in Vancouver that comes close to a fine dining and aesthetic experience for adults as well. The food is healthy but not grainy, with lots of kidfood like peanut butter sandwiches and chocolate-coated bananas. For adults: stuffed croissants, hefty burgers, a decent salmon en crout and well-stocked wine bar. There is an indoor play station with toys, colouring materials and headphones for listening to music. In summer you can sit at a patio table and let the kids splash around a few metres away in the Waterpark—Vancouver's most creative fair-weather playground.

You can't go to Isadora's every week, so here's a rundown of your best alternatives: Still on Granville Island, your kids will enjoy snacking at the **Blue Parrot** in the Public Market (1669 Johnston, west wing) where they can watch people strolling, gulls diving and boats sailing past the picture windows.

I have mixed feelings about the relatively new but wildly popular **Chuck E. Cheese** right next to the Lougheed Mall in Burnaby (9898 Government Place, 421-8408). I find when all the other senses are bombarded the appetite gets lost in the shuffle. The six-foot rodent (Big C to his pals) meets you at the door of this $2 million junkfood-and-video emporium, ushering you in to a space-age playground, games arcade, giant screen TV room and "Pizza Time Theatre" starring bands of roving computerized stuffed-animal musicians. Your kids will think they've arrived at heaven's gate.

The Old Spaghetti Factory in Gastown (53 Water, 684-1288) may be bland to your tastes but the transplanted streetcar, the old barber chairs and non-stop Three Stooges movies are guaranteed to keep your kids entertained while they slurp.

Victoria Station (1414 Hornby, 687-7511) strikes a better compromise, with a decent children's menu plus truly edible adult food. (Try the prime rib.) The railway car seating is a cute gimmick, and so is the menu that folds up into a train.

The White Spot (20 locations) is a notch above drive-in food, and no matter what damage they do to a veal cutlet you can't argue with the way they treat your kids. Lots of clever gimmicks—like fish and chips that comes in a pirate ship. You had best stick with the burgers and sandwiches.

Ethnic restaurants are almost always good for kids, especially Chinese, Italian and Mexican. No one even blinks when you ask for two boosters and a highchair—it's done all the time. One Mexican cafe that comes highly recommended by a friend with a very active two-year-old is **El Mexicano** (2052 Kingsway, 874-3232) where a strolling musician kept the little guy entertained for an hour.

If you're looking for a cheap feed, the **Hungry Bear** (2228 Main, 873-5587) has a passable fast-food menu and a special deal for kids—they pay according to age. Lunch is 35¢ per year, dinner is 50¢. And of course there is always **McDonald's.** The best ones I have found for entertainment value are at 1527 and 4455 Main where they have indoor merry-go-rounds and other small scale amusements for the under three, and at 3450 Hastings where you will find an enormous indoor playground suitable for the three and over. Grin and bear it.

Kid Culture

Do I see some kids moping behind a rain-washed window? Don't they know what's happening in the theatres, libraries, bookstores, concert halls and galleries all over the city? And a lot of it for free? Kids shouldn't be bored just because it's raining.

Showtime

The **Vancouver East Cultural Centre** (1895 Venables, 254-9578) plays host to some of the best children's entertainers in the country, including Sharon, Lois & Bram, Fred Penner, Green Thumb Players and Raffi. These big shows are usually on Sunday afternoons (call for the line-up); kids' films run Saturdays at 1 p.m. on a pay-what-you can basis.

Carousel and **Green Thumb Players,** Vancouver's two professional theatre companies for children, perform mostly in the schools but do special public performances on weekends and holidays, usually at VECC or **The Waterfront Theatre,** 1512 Anderson St. on Granville Island. Watch the papers. Carousel also hosts a weekly matinee performance of local clowns, mime artists and musicians called **Something Every Saturday** at The Waterfront. Call 683-9373 for details.

The cultural big leagues for little folks is definitely **The Sun Family Pops** series presented at the **Orpheum** by the Vancouver Symphony Orchestra (tickets and information from VTC outlets, 687-4444). Shows are usually on Sunday afternoons, featuring the orchestra fronted by guest artists like Sesame Street's Bob McGrath and guest companies like Vancouver's Axis Mime or Victoria's Kaleidoscope. You get a lot of show for the money—$6.50 to $10 for children, $10 to $15 for adults, less if you subscribe to the whole series.

Presentation House in North Vancouver (333 Chesterfield, 986-1351) has free family-oriented films every Sunday at 11 a.m. as well as varied weekend performances by visiting theatre companies. A similar mix of entertainment is staged at Burnaby's **James Cowan Theatre** (6450 Gilpin, Century Park, 291-6864) every Saturday at 1 p.m. The movies here cost $1.25 (adults $2.50) but you really get the cream—the best of Disney, George Lucas and sci-fi classics.

A number of the Vancouver community centres have weekend movies (**Douglas Park's** 75¢ movie-and-popcorn deal at 1:30 Saturdays is one of the most popular, 876-3371) but young connoisseurs keep one eye on the Sunday matinee schedule at the **Ridge** (16th and

Arbutus, 738-6311). The *Black Stallion, Watership Down, Lord of the Rings, Popeye*—you can trust Vancouver's rerun czar Leonard Schein to bring in the gems. The glass-enclosed crying room in the loges sounds like a great idea until you try to sit through a whole movie in there taking punishment not only from your own baby but from a dozen others.

Some people figure the most comfortable place to see a movie, especially on a rainy day, is their own living room. Impromptu video matinee parties happen wherever you get the combination of idle kids and an idle video cassette recorder. If you don't have a VCR you'll be surprised how inexpensive they are to rent—as low as $5 for the machine plus a movie every Tuesday at **Videomatica** (1829 West 4th, 734-0411). Other days it costs $7.50, or two movies for $5 if you already have the VCR at home.

It's a little more expensive, but if you're fussy about picture quality and selection, consider renting a video machine and movies on disc, $10 for the gear plus two movies at **Kits Video** (2164 West 4th, 738-3289) which has some 50 titles for kids.

Special Places and Events

A space-age adventure awaits kids at the **Arts, Sciences and Technology Centre** (600 Granville, 687-8414) where three floors of exhibits explore some serious subjects in a very playful manner. Conduct experiments on the colour wall, get into the giant math puzzles, do your own psycho-motor testing or play with the lasermaze. Exhibits change periodically, including fine arts and crafts. Schedule changes seasonally.

It isn't easy to interest kids in art, but the new **Vancouver Art Gallery** (750 Hornby, 682-5621) does a pretty good job in a mini-gallery devoted to children. If you are one of the 3,000 parents, grandparents and godparents who prepaid a $5 children's membership back in 1979 when the gallery was fundraising for this grand renovation, your kids will have the thrill of seeing their names lit up in coloured plexiglass at the entrance. The art inside can be a bit of an anti-climax, but VAG staff is on hand to act as animateurs, initiating discussion of the multi-media displays taken from the gallery's permanent collection. Fantasy, history and famous people are themes explored at this mini-gallery. Admission is free for under six, $1 for students and $2 for adults. Open Tuesday through Sunday.

The city's most special event for both youngsters and

escorts is the annual **Vancouver Children's Festival,** usually the first week in May. The best children's theatre, music, mime and puppetry from Canada and abroad is staged in giant tents at Vanier Park on Kits Point. Smart kids get their tickets early (they go on sale in early March, 687-7697) but you can usually squeeze into a show at the last minute by lining up outside the tent. Wear gumboots.

International films of interest to children and teenagers are showcased early each October during the **Vancouver International Children's Film Festival** at Robson Square (980-7933). Somewhat lighter fare is featured at the annual **Festival of Fools** (736-0797), a week-long revelry of mime and clowning that starts April 1 (naturally) with a parade on Granville Island and continues at The Waterfront Theatre.

Books and Storytime

Vancouver now has a bookstore dedicated entirely to children—**Kidsbooks** (2868 West 4th, 738-5335). Not only has Phyllis Simon stocked her shop with a large selection of top-quality books, she has designed the space in a way that makes browsing a joy for young and old. While you peruse the shelves, your kids can keep busy on the slide, rocking horse or in the toy chest. There is a proper change room with table, musical mobile and free diapers. Books range from pre-natal texts to teen fiction, and the week's highlight is the 2 p.m. program each Saturday featuring well-known singers, writers and magicians.

The best general bookstores for children's selections are **Duthie Books** (three locations), **Blackberry Books** on Granville Island (1663 Duranleau, 685-4113), **Woodward's Books** at Oakridge (41st at Cambie, 261-3311) and **Hager Books** (2176 West 41st, 263-9412). For secondhand kids' books, try **Mcleod's** (455 West Pender, 681-7654) where Don Stewart has thoughtfully provided a spacious kids' corner with table and chairs.

When it comes to the pre-school set, your neighbourhood library can be a more valuable resource than bookstores. **Vancouver Public Library** operates a wide range of free programs in all its branches, from story-telling for infants to book clubs for reluctant readers. A program guide comes out every three months (contact head children's librarian Janice Douglas, 665-3554) and VPL encourages parents to sign their kids up for regular weekly sessions at their local branch. But if you don't want to commit yourself in advance, you can usually drop in. Call ahead to make sure there is space.

Probably the most popular of VPL's programs is **Babytime,** a 25-minute story-telling session for three to 23 month olds, utilizing songs, puppets and fingerplay. Similar programs go right up to pre-schoolers with added sophistication at each level. Although the leaders are highly regarded at most of the branches, the physical set-up is best at Kits, Oakridge, Britannia and Mount Pleasant branches where kids can snuggle up in carpeted story pits.

INDOOR OUTINGS

Reclamation & Recreation

I suspect there are still at least a handful of people in Vancouver who haven't jumped onto the reclamation and rehabilitation bandwagon. I'm talking about bodies, of course. Fitness. This section is for those tardy few. The rest of you already have your running/swimming/aerobic/racquetball regimen down to a science. You can move directly on to the next section (your just reward)—After Dark.

For rainy-day convenience, I am focusing on sports and fitness centres that offer a variety of choices under one roof. One-stop fitness shopping, if you will. I mean, if you are making the grand effort to leave your cozy armchair to leap gazelle-like into a draughty gymn, the least you can do to recompense your weary body is immerse it in a warm whirlpool before hitting the wet pavement.

I am not including precise times or rates because these tend to fluctuate so rapidly I would only succeed in confusing or misleading you. The best idea is to call before you go. Also be sure to ask what facilities are available so you can be sure to bring the right gear.

Fitness Plus

The price is usually right at the Y, and thanks to stiff competitive pressure the facilities are pretty decent, even in the older buildings. In fact, a lot of people prefer the old **YMCA** (955 Burrard, 681-0221) precisely because it retains a hint of the old-style health club—the classic steam room, a judo room and (I love this) a snooze room. There is a pool, universal gymn plus roof-top jogging track with a nifty view of the downtown. For the past few years women have been admitted, but the atmosphere is pretty well male.

A more mixed crowd congregates at noon and after five at the **PenderWest Y** (1285 West Pender, third floor, 669-1196) where you'll find everything but a pool. There's a nicely varied aerobic workout schedule, plus weight training clinics. Waterproofed joggers take off from here into Stanley Park for the popular seawall circuit (there is a huge map of the park and pathways hanging in PenderWest) while the dry set do their cardio-vascular workout on a jogger's treadmill.

The **YWCA Fitness Centre** (580 Burrard, 683-2531) offers a great variety of fitness, dance and aquatics classes on a session or drop-in basis, with the added benefit of inexpensive babysitting. Some of the best prenatal fitness classes in the city are offered here, in gymn and pool. Instruction at the Y is generally friendly and competent enough. (Instructors are mostly volunteer.)

Local community centres offer inexpensive drop-in fitness classes, ideal for those who want to be broken in gently to the world of flab fighting. There are a lot of novices at these classes. But daily drop-in schedules are convenient for residents as well as visitors to Vancouver, and the community centres also offer the benefit of reputable child minding while you're grinding.

Fun is relative when you're talking about fitness. You do have to suffer, at least a little, to be beautiful. But the slick commercial centres put so much energy, imagination and money into entertaining the sweating masses that it takes mere days to transform a creaking, groaning novice into an aerobics junkie who gleefully shrieks "go for it" at the least provocation. It happened to me.

I'm now a regular at **The Fitness Group** (centres in Kitsilano and West Vancouver, 738-4169/926-8588) where you pay through the nose but you get results through your whole body. Director Barbara Crompton and her army of instructors are so incredibly good at what they do, and so totally up all the time that you can't help letting a little of their spirit rub off on you.

Crompton's biggest competitor in town is **Ron Zalko** (studios in Kitsilano and North Vancouver, 736-0341/986-3487) who may not be as strong on the interpersonal side but is leagues ahead in high tech. He has state-of-the-art sound systems and giant screens for video shows of his gorgeous wife/model/partner Dana (former Miss Israel) demonstrating the workout routines. Conservative jocks tend to favour The Fitness Group; the swingers go to Zalko.

But we have strayed from our intent. Neither of these have pools or alternative facilities for the one-stop fitness shopper. When I want the works, I drop in to one of **Bogie's Fitness Classes** at the Westin Bayshore's health club (1601 Georgia, 261-1319). David (Bogie) Bogoch offers high-calibre, upbeat workouts in a variety of locations, but the best deal by far is his Bayshore class. For the usual drop-in fee you get Bogie's muscular strength and endurance class plus access to all the indoor health club facilities—pool, weight room, whirlpool, showers, towel service, juice and snack bar and the services of resident masseur Stan Lis. Call 682-3377 to book your date with Stan, a body builder and former Mr. Poland.

If you have the courage to face the facts about your state of fitness, you can make a special date to meet Bogie here for a personalized evaluation of your cardiovascular system, muscular strength, endurance, flexibility, even your daily diet. Bogie leaves nothing to chance. It is a gruelling but most informative 90-minute fitness test, followed by a detailed written evaluation and return appointment to chart your plan of action. The whole package cost me $30 plus the use of my arms and legs for 24 hours.

Racquets Plus

The best you can get on a drop-in basis is the **Super Court Racquet Centre** (6311 B Westminster Hwy, Richmond, 278-4571) which is a fair way to drive for a 45-minute game. But then, court deprivation has driven people further than that. There are three squash and seven racquetball courts available seven days a week, 6:45 a.m. to 11 p.m., with babysitting and saunas on the side. Prices are reasonable (about $8) considering the quality of the courts; community centre racquet facilities are cheaper but they seem to make up their own regulations for court size and construction.

Eventually, most racquet jocks come to terms with the fact that their addiction is going to cost them money, and they join a private club. The fancy places are downtown. At a centre like the **Bentall Racquet and Fitness Academy** (4 Bentall Centre, 595 Burrard, 689-4424) it will cost you close to $100 initiation, $300 annually plus between $8 and $12 an hour for a court. That buys you access to the Nautilus gymn plus a full range of physical and gastronomic indulgences. It's $150 less if you just want to play racquetball.

The only place in town that offers public pay-as-you go indoor tennis is the **Delta Airport Inn** (10251 St. Edwards, Richmond, 278-9611) where there are three courts, a 40-foot pool, sauna and whirlpool, weight room and quarter-mile jogging track. You pay only for the court—$10 to $13 an hour depending on time of day. Phone at least two days ahead to reserve.

Pools & Rinks

Vancouver is a serious swimming town, and most serious swimmers whom I know agree that the best indoor pool is at the **Vancouver Aquatic Centre** (1050 Beach,

689-7156). The 50-metre salt-water pool is beautifully designed for length swimming as well as splashing around. There is a separate teaching pool for kids plus sauna, whirlpool, diving tank and weight-training room. There are fitness classes on the pool deck three times a week, and excellent babysitting facilities for infants and toddlers.

UBC Aquatic Centre (call 228-4521 for directions into the campus) is a slightly smaller pool but is less crowded during the evening public swims than is its downtown counterpart. Daytime family swims on weekends are popular and do tend to get a bit frantic, but they're fun as a social splash. Keep-fit classes are offered five times a week, morning and evening.

Skating is best done on a schoolyard rink surrounded by snowdrifts with Viennese waltzes crackling through old speakers and woodsmoke from the rinkhouse fireplace pouring over the ice. Unfortunately this is Vancouver, not Saskatoon. The closest you can get to the old schoolyard rinks is at the community centres.

There are public rinks at six different community centres. One of the largest and most popular is the **Kerrisdale Arena** (5670 East Boulevard, 261-8144) where there is a varied schedule of parent-and-tot, adult-only, drop-in hockey and family skate throughout the week. You can book the arena for private skating parties Saturday evenings, about $65 for two hours. Reasonably priced skate rentals are available, including skid rails for tots.

You don't get the snow drifts, the woodsmoke or the Viennese waltzes, but **Robson Square** offers outdoor skating on the small sheltered rink in the centre of the sunken courtyard (800 Hornby, 668-2830). It helps to be able to do a tight turn here, and to have a rear-view mirror strapped to your toque. If you're an exhibitionist, this is your rink. Bring your own skates, and Walkman—unless you want to pirouette to Muzak. There is usually ice from November through March, and although some people rollerskate here the rest of the year, it is not encouraged.

UBC's **Thunderbird Winter Sports Centre** (6066 Thunderbird Blvd., 228-6121) has the biggest public rink in Vancouver, but Physical Education students and amateur hockey leagues monopolize a large part of the schedule. Despite years of pressure, UBC has kept Friday evening and Sunday afternoons open for public skating.

This place is so big it never feels crowded: a pretty good facsimile of the great outdoors.

Curlers: You can rent a sheet at the Thunderbird rink for $15 to $20 an hour, if you can find one open. Weekday afternoons are your best bet, or weekends when there is no bonspiel.

Spectator Sports

There is only one place to start: **B.C. Place Stadium.** If you think this giant spaceship looks great from the outside, you should see it from the inside. In my opinion, the stadium makes the sports event. If you feel the same way you can save a lot of money by just taking a stadium tour and forgetting about the event. Groups meet at Gate A (777 Taylor St.) daily at 11 a.m., 1 and 3 p.m for a guided one-hour tour. Special seniors and handicapped groups meet Tuesdays, Thursdays and Sundays at 1:30 p.m. Adults $2.75, seniors and students $2, children $1.25, group rate $2 per person (call 661-3664 to book groups).

B.C. Place Stadium Events

(For all B.C. Place Events information and ticket sales, call Vancouver Ticket Centre, 687-1818.)

Sports fans are a fickle lot. A couple of year ago the hottest action in town was soccer, but since we hosted the Grey Cup in '83 (and it looks like we've got it again in '86) the fever is football. If you are lucky enough to get your hands on them, tickets to the **B.C. Lions'** 10 CFL games, June through November, run $9 to $18 each, no discounts for seniors or children.

The **Vancouver Whitecaps** (NASL soccer) play at the stadium April through September, and just for confusion's sake they call it the "Outdoor Season" to distinguish it from the "Indoor Season" at the Pacific Coliseum, December to March. The Whitecaps play once or twice a week at B.C. Place, charging $9 to $13 with discounts for seniors, students and B.C. Soccer Association members.

Major league baseball comes to the stadium only during exhibition season in March, when crowds pack the place to see the big-time American players. Our own **Triple A Canadians** can't afford the stadium rent, which is just as well if you talk to the die-hard fans who brave the elements to root for them in the old-fashioned **Nat Bailey Stadium** (see About Town, below).

Jimmy Connors and his fellow stars on the international tennis circuit show up every October for a six-day stadium tournament. It is a crowd pleasing event, but real tennis aficionados like to get a lot closer to the play at the smaller club tournaments. Schedule information available from the **B.C. Tennis Association,** 687-3333.

They had ball games in mind when they built the stadium, but its versatility really shines when they host events like **Supercross Festival,** usually in late fall and early spring. Some 750 truckloads of dirt are dumped on the stadium floor and sculpted into a track for the bikes and the Formula 10 racing cars. Tickets are about $12 to $14. It's a noisy, raunchy show—but subdued compared to the summer/winter **Tractor Pull** event where Hell's Angels mingle with the mom-and-pop crowd from Surrey to watch super-souped farm machinery move mountains of dirt around the stadium. The people who live in False Creek across the bridge from B.C.Place still remember the time they fired up the jet-propelled tractor. The value of their real estate went down 10 percent.

PNE Events

Of course the most obvious attraction at the PNE grounds (Hastings at Renfrew) is the **Pacific National Exhibition** itself, the last two weeks of August. Kids go for Playland, revellers go for the beer gardens, homebodies go for the home show, city folk and farm folk alike go for the prize livestock, poultry and horse shows, little ones love the petting zoo and big ones love the food pavilion. Everything but the midway is sheltered, and if you ask me, you don't miss a thing staying indoors. Admission to the fair is $3 adults, $1 children under 12, free for children under six. Details: 253-2311.

A word about parking at the PNE: During the fair and major sports events, be prepared for a wet hike from on-street parking into the pavilions and stadiums. There are public parking lots ($2) but you can wait in line forever to get a spot. Your best bet is to take the bus—#14 Hastings or #16 Renfrew northbound from Granville and Davie, downtown; during the PNE in late August look for the #14 Hastings - PNE Express or the #9 Broadway - PNE Express eastbound at Broadway and Granville.

Another big draw is **Exhibition Park horse racing,** early April to mid-October. Parade to post is 6:15 Monday, Wednesday and Friday: 1:15 Saturdays, Sundays and holidays. Aside from the hike into the grandstand, you can stay perfectly dry wherever you station yourself at the track. The grandstand is covered but not enclosed, so your $2.50 admission to the cheap seats will buy you a draughty evening in early and late season. It is more comfortable (though some argue less real) in the clubhouse, admission $4.50, which is almost entirely enclosed. The track people are quite proud of their dining-room food (your basic roast beef/salmon steak fare served up on fine china and white linen) but if you want to watch the races rather than just the video monitors, you're better off eating more casually in the Table Terrace, $3.25 extra. To reserve a table there, call 254-1631 exactly a week before you want to go, at post time. The terrace is extremely popular and not very big, so tables go fast. If the food matters to you, stay in the dining room where the menu is much more varied. And don't miss the lavish Sunday smorgasbord.

Major indoor sports events at the PNE grounds include the **Vancouver Canucks** hockey season September to April with play-offs April and May, $11 to $17 for tickets, no discounts (254-5141); the **Whitecaps Indoor Soccer** season is December through March, $6 to $8, discounts (291-6661); professional boxing has an erratic schedule at the **Coliseum** (253-2311), depending on fight promoters, and ticket prices are equally erratic—$30 to $200 for prizefighters like Spinks.

Wrestling is a much more regular affair at the PNE, with the "All Stars" almost every other Monday night at **The Gardens,** tickets at door (253-2311); and the popular Stampede Wrestling from Calgary about once a month at the larger **Agrodome,** tickets at VTC (687-1818). Admission to wrestling is about $7. Dust off all your old cat-calls for these matches.

While you're at the PNE (worth a special trip for sports fans) drop into the **B.C. Sports Hall of Fame** (253-2311) at the B.C. Pavilion, close to the main gates at Hastings and Renfrew. Open weekdays only, 9:15 a.m. to 4:15 p.m., this mini-museum traces the history and development of virtually all sports through photos, scrapbooks and mementos. There is a picture gallery of Hall of Fame members, and an amazing collection of Olympic, Pan American and Commonwealth Games medals. Great for sports-crazed kids.

About Town

If B.C. Place is a spaceship, **Nat Bailey Stadium** (4601 Ontario) is an apple pie—and what better metaphor for the home of Vancouver's only professional baseball team, the **Triple A-league Canadians** (872-5232). "It's the old, down home, American ballpark," is how sports writer Jim Christie describes the place, railing against big-dome baseball in towns like Seattle where fans end up watching the video monitors more than the game. Writer Sean Rossiter enthusiastically agrees: "The joy of baseball is the sunlight, the real grass, real dirt and the real city view beyond the outfield fence." (It's truly a million-dollar view from Bailey Stadium which perches on the side of Little Mountain.)

The Canadians play something like 72 home games from early April through August. On a clear day the $5.50 box seats right down by the field are the best places to be, but if it's raining go for the reserved (covered) section of the grandstand, $5; kids and seniors $2.50.

Now that posh racquet centres are mushrooming all over town, lounge lizards can get into serious spectator sports without getting off the sofa. The trendy place to have a light dinner, a drink and watch the tournament finals is the **Inn at Denman Place** (1733 Comox, 688-7711). This is the squash club of repute in Vancouver (there is also racquetball, but less popular) and if you prefer to watch than play, you can just saunter in any time during one of the big contests.

The **Vancouver Open Squash Tournament** takes

place here every February, but bigger still is the **Denman Open** on the Halloween weekend with a wind-up party that blows the roof off. There is a Denman Open for racquetball at the same time, so between the two there are about 500 participants, guests and onlookers at the bash. The prestige clubs like Denman, **Supreme Courts** (1114 Alberni, 669-3636) and **Chancery Place** (847 Hornby, 682-3752) have closed-circuit videos in their lounges so you don't have to strain yourself looking down into the courts from your sofa. Squash pro Shane Vincent and racquetball pro Annie May at the Denman Inn Racquet Centre are good contacts for all local tournament dates and times. 688-7711

To Market

Remember when the height of decadence in grocery shopping was phoning in your list to the corner grocer and having the lot delivered? No muss, no fuss, no waste of precious time squeezing through tables of tomatoes or waiting for your chuck roast to be ground. Today's connoisseurs wouldn't dream of letting someone else squeeze their tomatoes or sniff their salmon, which is why the old-style farmers' markets have made such a comeback.

People have gone back to grocery shopping with a vengeance, willing to spend the better part of a Saturday afternoon prodding through produce to find the absolute freshest available. In fact, we've gone so nuts about freshness many of us will head for the market to pass an hour or two even if we don't need any groceries. We'll ponder an ice-tray of fresh prawns the way an art connoisseur ponders a great painting. So when we discuss markets here as rainy-day destinations, you have to understand we're looking at them as galleries—freshness on exhibition.

Granville Island Public Market

It is hard to say whether the new interest in fresh foods sparked the market trend or whether the development of markets like the one on Granville Island (1669 Johnston, 685-6577) created the interest. One thing is for sure: Granville Island can take credit for at least half the great dinner parties held in Vancouver in the past two years.

Here is how a ho-hum grocery list can grow into the makings for a Bon Appetit dinner party when the shopping is being done at the Public Market: You're on the lookout for salad fixings when you notice Ernie Rahn has managed to get some Belgian endive in at his **Island City Farm** stand. You go into automatic pilot, your mouth already watering in anticipation of the cold marinated mussels you're going to stuff the leaves with (you find them at **Market Seafood** where you save time by also picking up the whole Sockeye which they've butterfly-filetted for free) and the fresh watercress **(Duso's)** and the lemon wedges to garnish them. It's payday, so why not spring for a truffle or two to thinly slice on top (for $1 a gram at **La Madrague** you're looking at thin) and while you're at this tantalizing French butcher shop why not take some of that feather-light salmon mousse?

Back down to earth over at **The Granary,** you'd better stock up on long-grain rice and a sprinkling of pine nuts, then go across the aisle to **Attilio's Pasta Net** for fresh-grated Parmesan to top the vegetables (spiced sauteed kohlrabi for a change, with leeks and red pepper from **Fraser Valley Farms.**) If it's summer, an amazing variety of dessert fruit surrounds you. If it's winter, look for Norman Groblacher's **Rainbow King** stand (he's a day tenant so he moves around; just ask someone who works there). He flies in plump, ripe Hawaiian delicacies like papaya, pineapple and giant avocados.

But for the real delicacies—crunchy/chewy baguettes, chocolate truffles and brie that make all others taste like imitations—leave the market through the central door on Johnston, cross the road and head into **La Baguette et L'Echalotte.** This is the second gourmet shop of Louise Turgeon and Mario Armitano, who started with La Madrague in the market. No one has a nose for cheese like Mario or a sense for sauce like Louise. Their baking and sweets are also exceptional. I understand there are customers who wandered in when La Baguette first opened in 1982 and are still there, trying to decide what to order.

Well there it is, your award-winning dinner. Granted, you could have saved a bundle by going out to a fine restaurant—but it wouldn't have been half the fun.

If you aren't bothered by the press of human flesh and the crush of car bumpers, you'll enjoy the market any time. But if you want to take it at a more relaxing pace, head down on a week day, or as close as possible to the 9 a.m./6 p.m. opening and closing on weekends. You will be able to tell as soon as you enter the causeway just how bad the congestion is, and if it looks heavy, take a quick exit onto one of the side streets and park there. Believe me, you'll save time and aggravation walking onto the island, even in the rain, rather than competing in the bumper-car race for parking spots nearer the markets.

Even better, avoid the thoroughfares altogether by catching the **False Creek Ferry** (see Cruising: Land, Sea & Air, page 12) which crosses between downtown and the island several times an hour, year round. The ferry is inconvenient only for shoppers laden with bags full of market produce.

While you're on Granville Island, if it isn't raining too hard, take a bit of a walk. We're not talking distance here—circumference of the whole island takes under an hour. The so-called island tucked under Granville Bridge is actually attached by a narrow causeway accessible from West 4th if you're coming from the west. An industrial slum until recently, the land has been redeveloped and the old factories and warehouses recycled (with something still of the industrial look) by $20 million from the federal government. Corrugated metal has taken on bright primary-coloured paint, chunky wooden lamp standards have been revived and high-tech architecture added to enhance the mood.

It is fun, funky and (this is the only hitch) very popular. (For more on Granville Island galleries, see Art Tour, page 46; for restaurants, clubs and lounges see The High Life, page 104 and Lingering over Lunch, page 112.)

Outlying Markets

If the crush of Granville Island is more than you're willing to tolerate for freshness, there are two very down-to-earth markets in New Westminster that you ought to visit. They are open weekends only, and the best time to hit the stands (as at all real farmers' markets) is first thing in the morning.

At the **City Market** (1051 Columbia St., New West, 521-4616) first thing means as close to 7 a.m. on Fridays and Saturdays as you can make it. I know it's tough on a dark, wet winter morning, but if you get there later than 9 a.m. a lot of the goods are picked over. Mind you, the atmosphere stays just fine right through to the 1 p.m. closing. This is a colourful old barn of a market, with original 1930s murals on the walls and a homey, craftsy feeling throughout. Besides fresh produce you can buy home-cured meats, good old-fashioned baking and all kinds of crafts. You won't find Granville Island's fancy cappuccinos or Vietnamese crab-roll snacks—coffee shop fare is strictly hamburgers, fries and muffins.

If you don't make it in time for the City Market despite every good intention, no need to despair. Down on the waterfront is the much larger **Fraser River Market** (236 Front St., New West, 520-6181) which has much saner hours: 9 a.m. to 8 p.m. Fridays, 9 to 5 Saturdays, Sundays and holidays. This place hasn't got quite as much character, but you can't complain about the goods. The 20,000-square-foot converted warehouse contains some 90 shops and stands, offering produce, fresh fish, meats, crafts and a fast food area where you can eat Greek, Chinese or Mexican style fastfood.

You can't get fish any fresher or cheaper than straight off the boat, which is how they sell them at the **Steveston Fishing Village** in southwest Richmond (Hwy. 99 south to Steveston Hwy., west to No. 2 Rd., south to Moncton St.). Hundreds of boats, from the old seiners to huge new processing ships, line the docks on weekends to unload their catch of salmon, snapper, sole, shrimp, prawns, crab—whatever is in season. Again, best time to get there is before 9 a.m. Comparison shopping will get you the best prices, and if you're lucky, a filetted and cleaned fish.

You can stock up on produce on your return trip through Richmond by heading for one of the many farm stands in the area. If it's berry season (late spring) and you've got your gumboots on, take Westminister Hwy. west from the 99 North and within feet of the interchange you'll see U-Pick signs for the cheapest, freshest berry deal in town. Many of the farm stands have U-Pick deals on various fruit and vegetables right through the growing season, but because few of them have phones you have to drive around and look. No. 5 and No. 6 roads running north-south are good bets, as well as Westminster Hwy. running east-west.

My choice is **Cherry Lane Fruit Farm** (9631 Bridgeport Rd.), because it's easy to get to (very close to the foot of the Oak St. bridge) and has one of the best selections—from filbert nuts to rutabagas. My mom, famous for her half-done kosher dills, gets her pickling cukes there.

Nature Under Cover

"What a shame," goes the common complaint. "Vancouver has so much natural beauty, but it's almost always too wet to enjoy." The complaint may be common, but it's certainly uneducated. Even on the most miserable winter days you can enjoy nature thanks to the numerous public and private efforts to capture it under a roof. At virtually every major outdoor attraction somebody has had the good sense to build an indoor monument, museum or nature centre to show off the best of our surroundings from a warm, dry vantage. Below are the half-dozen on top of my list.

The Vancouver Aquarium

The beluga and killer whale shows are the big draws at the **Vancouver Aquarium** (682-1118) in Stanley Park, but I prefer just wandering through the galleries filled with red-eared sliders swimming about in their ponds, wolf eels with crab-crunching jaws, crocodiles relentlessly staring the tourists down and tiny fragile seahorses darting through illuminated tanks along with the shockingly coloured Picasso triggerfishes. There are about 6,000 aquatic animals here along with their arboreal pals, like the two-toed sloths, and their air-borne buddies, like the multi-coloured Amazon parakeets and tufted puffins that "fly" through the water. After a dozen visits you will still see something new and surprising around every corner.

It is not hyperbole to say that The Vancouver Aquarium is one of the finest in the world and should not be missed. It's organized into sections—the **B.C. Hall of Fishes** featuring native species like the giant Pacific octopus, the **MacMillan Tropical Gallery** displaying an amazing variety of marine life from all tropical oceans, and the new **Graham Amazon Gallery** full of giant snakes, crazy birds, strange insects and frogs slithering about a jungle-like setting.

If you want to see a spectacle, catch one of the whale shows either from the poolside seats outside or the underwater windows which give you a terrific view of the thrust that propels these 8,000-pound animals straight out of the water. There are four killer shows a day, four beluga shows, plus two outdoor feedings of the sea otter family (the kids I regularly go with like these little fellows best). Shows are included in the admission price: $4.50 adults, $2.25 seniors and students, children under five free. Aquarium is open daily 10 a.m to 6 p.m. in summer, 10 to 5 in winter.

Capilano Salmon Hatchery

Speaking of fish, did you know some salmon make it most of the way to Japan before their homing instinct calls them back to the exact stream bed where they were born? And did you know that when young salmon are mature enough to handle life in the ocean, they automatically stop swimming upstream, do a U-turn and head downstream with the current? There are a lot more amazing salmon facts to be gleaned by visiting the

Capilano Hatchery (987-1411), an impressive cedar-and-glass structure which straddles the Capilano River just upstream from the famous suspension bridge (see page 39).

The salmonid enhancement process is so delicate that visitors are not allowed into the area where the sexually mature salmon and steelhead are killed, their eggs and sperm removed, eggs fertilized and incubated for 70 days. But you can see the fish ladder which helps the old guys get up the turbulent stream into the hatchery tanks, and you can go outside to view the ponds that are thick with silvery young graduates of this Capilano Private School for Fish. The in-between stages are extremely well illustrated in display cases.

The best time of year for fish population is September through November, after which the ladder crowd thins down to the odd straggler. But there are young fish in the ponds all year, except in June when they are released, and the displays are permanent. Admission is free; hours are 8 a.m to dusk daily. Get there by taking Capilano Road in North Vancouver, take the first left past the suspension bridge onto Capilano Park Road. The hatchery is 1.5 km. along.

Bloedel Conservatory

The illuminated triodetic dome that perches atop Little Mountain (33rd Ave. and Cambie) is not only a flower-lover's paradise, it is steamy balm to the body and mind—a tiny tropical holiday in the middle of the city. A winding path leads through floral gardens (magnificent orchids and other exotics bloom in March-April), under tree ferns and luxuriant palms and around to the arid gardens of cacti in shapes and colours that defy definition—though of course everything is scientifically classified for the serious botany buffs. The dome is filled with the shrieking, whistling and twittering of some 20 species of tropical birds.

If you are suitably dressed, finish your visit with a stroll through the lovely quarry gardens in Queen Elizabeth Park below the conservatory. Landscaped around sheer cliffs and waterfalls, the gardens are suitable for winter or summer strolling. But in spring the whole mountainside explodes into floral colour, provoking normally reserved guidebook writers to explode into effusive prose. Forgive me.

H.R. MacMillan Planetarium

The shows are good, but the seats are great. What

better way to wile away a rainy afternoon than in the comfort of a dentist's chair, but with the Milky Way instead of the dentist hovering over you? The planetarium, part of the Vancouver Museum complex at 1100 Chestnut on Kits Point, is a popular stop for tourists but sadly underutilized by natives. It's a shame that people may shy away from astronomy because of the "educational overtones;" the planetarium shows are not only a feast to the eye (the multi-image computerized projection system makes for highly sophisticated, creative effects) but also very entertaining for adults as well as young people.

The planetarium reaches a mixed audience these days, with the usual astronomy-related shows Tuesday through Sunday afternoons and evenings, $3 admission; the more whimsical fare geared to children and parents on weekend mornings; and the popular sound-and-light concerts Tuesday through Sunday nights, $4.25. For times and program information, call 736-4431.

MacMillan Bloedel Place

Three out of my list of six nature-oriented attractions bear the Mac-Blo name—testimony not only to a prudent PR department but also to the B.C. forestry giant's good intentions to return something to the people of the province in exchange for all the trees it cuts down. MacMillan Bloedel Place, located in the **VanDusen Botanical Display Gardens,** (5251 Oak, 263-2688) is really a gift from the company's heart. The attractive cedar-and-glass pavilion is nicknamed "A Walk in the Forest," which is precisely what is recreated in an indoor, educational context.

I find it gratifying to take this forest walk with at least one inquisitive kid on hand, so when he/she asks the predictable questions (how come leaves change colour? how does the water get all the way up to the top of the tree?) I can play All-Knowing by reading the answers. Unless you are a fairly serious botany buff, you might find this place dry. On the other hand, if you're out enjoying the natural bounty of VanDusen Gardens and a cloud bursts on you, here's a nice, dry place you can run to. There is no charge, except for the VanDusen gate fee of $1.50 for adults, seniors and children. Open daily 10 a.m. to dusk.

DAY DRIVES

If you have a car, you'll welcome the rain as a perfect excuse to settle in behind the wheel with your map (the best road map is *Greater Vancouver, Fraser Valley & Victoria,* $1.50 at kiosks and gas stations) and your dollar-bag of road mix (my own assortment: similar to trail mix but more cashews). Vancouver is so rich in scenic forest drives, mountain panoramas and sea vistas you can almost proceed in any direction and get an eyeful. But if you have limited time and want to pack the most scenery into a few hours' drive, consider these routes.

The Vancouver Special

I know people who were born and raised in Vancouver and still take all or part of this drive whenever they need to remind themselves how lucky they are not to be living in Sudbury, Ontario.

Start at Coal Harbour at the north foot of Denman Street, where West Georgia and Denman converge into the Stanley Park Causeway. Get into the right lane and stay there or you'll find yourself hurtling toward the Lions Gate Bridge (in which case just go for it—flipping quickly ahead to either the North Shore Special #1 or #2). The right lane takes you into Stanley Park which you'll circle via Park Drive. As you enter the park you'll see the Coal Harbour marinas on your right—Vancouver Rowing Club in front of the grand old Tudor house, the Royal Vancouver Yacht Club with its artistically-painted boat sheds and the Westin Bayshore Hotel across the harbour. By the way, the tiny lake you just passed with the tacky fountain (it looks better at night) is Lost Lagoon where there is such an overpopulation of waterfowl thanks to the overpopulation of crumb-throwing on-lookers. Every now and then traffic comes to an abrupt halt to let geese and goslings cross the busy causeway.

As you come round the first bend a spectacular view of Burrard Inlet surprises you. Take it slow (or better yet, get out of the car at the viewpoint lot) and note the Second Narrows Bridge to the east, Port of Vancouver and North Vancouver on either side, the Lions Gate Bridge to the west flanked by the massive bright yellow sulfur piles at Vancouver Wharves on one side and the mountainside residential community of West Vancouver on the other. Even on a cloudy day you can see most of Grouse Mountain to the northwest, Hollyburn northeast.

It is picture-postcard beautiful all the way around Park

Drive which carves through a rare bit of urban old-growth forest—towering Douglas fir, western red cedar and arbutus. If you want to savour the view, stop for tea or lunch at the elegant **Ferguson Point Tea House** (669-3281; ask for a seat in the arboretum). There is a casual coffee shop at **Prospect Point** where you can munch a muffin and ponder the legacy of the "Beaver," pioneer steamship of the Pacific that was wrecked on these same rocks in 1888. There is also a cafeteria and proper restaurant at **The Beach House** (681-9951) on the south stretch of the drive where you can have French fare and fine wine or fish-and-chips with a pint before heading out of the park onto Beach Ave.

Beach Avenue is serious strolling territory, with the Miami-pink and blue apartments on your left, English Bay Beach on your right and Kits Point marked by the planetarium across the water. There are generally half a dozen great cargo ships anchored in the mouth of the bay. Beach turns into Pacific which takes you (right) onto Burrard Bridge. Stay right, take the turn-off onto Cornwall, and make another sharp right immediately onto Cypress. Proceed straight toward the totem pole if you want to keep driving, or turn at the green sign for a stop at the **Maritime Museum,** the **Vancouver Museum** (see Historical Tour, page 48), or the **H.R. MacMillan Planetarium** (see Nature Under Cover, page 92).

Take a left at the totem pole and hug Kitsilano Beach Park until you find yourself back on Cornwall, which soon turns into Point Grey. Water views on your right are replaced by lovely homes whose inhabitants keep the view to themselves—but fortunately only for a mile or so. Follow the Scenic Drive signs left on Alma to West 4th and turn right again past Jericho Beach Park which turns into Locarno and then Spanish Banks. By now you are about even with the ships at anchor, and if you're into ship-gazing you can stop at one of the beach-front parking lots. Or keep driving, noting how the houses on the hill make way for the forests of the University Endowment Lands which in turn make way for the impeccably trimmed hedges of even more beautiful houses. (Numerous trails lead off the road, up the cliffs of the U.E.L. forests or down to the beaches.)

Keep turning right when you get to the U.B.C. campus, and if you are ready for a leg stretch, watch on your right for signs to the **Museum of Anthropology**—a stunning cliffside monument to the Northwest Coast Indians (Historical Tour, page 49). U.B.C.'s 110 acres of gardens, the Japanese **Nitobe Memorial Gardens** (Gore-Tex and Gumboots, page 40) in particular, are not to be missed.

Closet dragsters will appreciate the divided highway that takes you around the backside of the campus, onto South West Marine Drive. Your water view is now the mouth of the Fraser River, virtually covered with a patchwork of log booms. Stop at the historical marker/viewpoint for a quick lesson on explorer Simon Fraser who opened the river as a supply system for the Hudson Bay Company in 1808.

The next stop for serious river watchers is **Celtic Shipyards,** reached by taking Blenheim St. right from Marine (at the Point Grey Golf and Country Club). This sheltered inlet is packed with colourful fishing vessels and tugs.

Continuing along Marine eastward we begin the awesome home-gazing portion of our tour. Only problem is, you have to really crane your neck around the hedges to see the fine old plums that perch on the Fraser bank between Yew and Angus. This is not just a homes tour but a who's who of Vancouver, then and now. Among the notables: Canfor lumber magnate Peter Bentley's Tudor giant (2206) built in the 1920s by B.C. Sugar tycoon Benjamin Tingley Rogers; Rio Vista (2170), a delightful Spanish wedding cake with red tile icing, built in 1931 by one of the Carling-O'Keefe beer brothers, Harry Reifel, now inhabited by the ubiquitous Joe Segal (The Bay, Field's, Zellers); The Gables (2106) built in 1929 by B.C. Electric industrialist William Murrin, later purchased by Victor MacLean, a grandson of Kelly Douglas food magnate Robert Kelly; the Frank McMahon estate (2010), originally belonging to the sugar family Rogers; the grand old Malkin Estate (1950), a French Regency mansion built in 1925 by food wholesaler Fred Malkin and later bought by department store magnate Chunky Woodward; and right next door (1920) Casa Mia, a Spanish revival mansion to rival Harry Reifel's, built in 1931 by brother George Reifel on a seven-acre lot.

Want to see more nice shacks? Your tour concludes with a northward drive down Granville St. which you can pick up just after the last mansion on Marine. (Follow signs to Granville, north.) It is a few miles' drive north to **Shaughnessy,** the very heart of Old Money Vancouver. You can tour it by turning down almost any street between 33rd and 16th, but if you want a concentrated 10-minute tour take Angus Dr. right (Angus is four blocks north of 25th). This grand boulevard takes you onto **The Crescent,** an even grander circular street around a boulevard park. (There's more on this part of town in Umbrella Tours, p. 33.) Take Angus back onto Granville, and you are just a few minutes from the bridge back into the downtown.

The North Shore Specials:

North Shore Special #1

This tour heads toward Deep Cove, the picturesque bedroom community perched on the cliffs overhanging Indian Arm at the east end of Burrard Inlet. Getting there from Vancouver is as much a treat as being there, especially if you are game to climb out of your car and enjoy a couple of roadside parks that lend themselves nicely to rainy-day visits.

If you start your drive from the Lions Gate Bridge, keeping right to veer onto the North Vancouver/Marine Drive exit, you will come to the first park after a five km. drive due east. (Marine turns into 3rd St. and then into Cotton Rd.) **Park and Tilford Gardens** (1200 Cotton, 987-9321) has a most unusual system of covered pathways that shelter you as you wander through exquisitely manicured mini-gardens—roses, herbs, rhododendrons, native flora, an Oriental display, a greenhouse full of tropicals and an aviary housing exotic parrots and (in summer) an amazing variety of finches.

These gardens are most famous at Christmastime for the ornamental display, but you can lift your spirits here any time of year, especially if you make a stop at the adjacent Spirit Shop run by the Park and Tilford Distillery. Open daily 8 a.m. to 11 p.m.

Alternately, head for the North Shore by way of the Second Narrows Bridge, drive east to Nanaimo St. in Vancouver, then turn north. A number of different routes will get you to Nanaimo, but I prefer skirting the north shore of False Creek, passing the Expo 86 site, the domed stadium, and following the Bypass Expressway from Pacific to Hastings, then east to Nanaimo. Stay in the right bridge lane to make a hasty exit to Deep Cove, on Dollarton Highway.

The high arched span of the Second Narrows Bridge affords one of the finest panoramas of Vancouver. The Lions Gate gives you the serene vista of English Bay opening out into the Strait of Georgia, but this bridge gives you a sense of what Vancouver is all about—a city on the banks of a bustling harbour.

Dollarton is not much of a "highway"—more like a two-lane road winding along the bank of Burrard Inlet, offering fine views of the still water and forested hillside rising on its south bank. (Even the small refineries look inoffensive in this idyllic setting.) About five km. east of the bridge is the sign to **Cates Park.**

There are no covered walkways here, but if you don't mind getting a tad damp you won't regret braving your way into this misty, enchanted little park. In the fall maple leaves carpet the narrow entrance road, and in spring wild flowers are everywhere. There is a boat launch with sheltered picnic tables nearby, and further east a meticulously kept grass lawn circled in forest. There is a small clearing affording the kind of still, contemplative view that makes you want to sit down (there are benches) and write verse. Novelist Malcolm Lowry, who lived nearby, must have done some deep contemplating here because they named a beautiful forest trail after him. Kdis will like exploring the mossy remains of a sawmill, checking out the totem poles and an amazing hand-carved 50-foot war canoe, or burning off steam at the adventure playground which is largely sheltered by forest.

Dollarton Highway leads onto Deep Cove Road shortly after the park, taking you into the hillside town. Stay on the road straight through to **Panorama Park** on the bluff over Deep Cove Marina. The park lives up to its name. Gazing at the incredibly still inlet surrounded by woods rising to steep mountains, you won't believe you are in Greater Vancouver—just 20 minutes from the bank towers and malls. There are sheltered picnic tables here, a stone's throw from the pizza takeouts and donut shops of Gallant Ave. If you are by now hungry enough for a serious meal, the restaurant of repute is **The Savoury** (929-2373), featuring a wide-ranging continental menu, $12 to $18 for entrees. The rack of lamb in mustard sauce comes highly recommended.

If it is still daylight and the cloud cover is high, your return trip might include a drive up **Mount Seymour** for views that will make Panorama Park look like puddle gazing. You can get onto the Mount Seymour Parkway from Deep Cove Rd. about one km. from the cove marina, and take the road up to the alpine area another one km. along. There are a number of viewpoints along the 1,000-metre elevation, the first of which (Vancouver Lookout) gives you a spectacular slice of the city and surrondings even on a medium-cloudy day. The second

(Deep Cove Lookout) is eight km. up and definitely worth the drive on a light-cloudy day. On a clear day you can pretty well see forever by proceeding to the alpine base level.

Take the Mount Seymour Parkway back to Dollarton Highway. Signs lead you easily onto the Second Narrows Bridge to Vancouver or west along Marine Drive through North Vancouver to the Lions Gate Bridge. Game for more driving? Keep on going via...

North Shore Special #2

By now you can make your own way over the **Lions Gate Bridge.** Go straight off the bridge onto the wide-sweeping turnabout leading to Marine Drive and West Vancouver—a gem of a mountainside community that reacted early on to the heavily industrial development of neighbouring North Vancouver by virtually banning industry. Early in the century the West Van town fathers further decided to set high standards for residential development by prohibiting lots less than 75 feet wide. The right developers were attracted—including a British group, led by the Guiness (beer) family, who in 1932 formed British Pacific Properties Ltd. and started carving up the slopes of Hollyburn Ridge rising to your right from Marine Dr.

Today **British Properties** is on every tour guide's agenda. (See Ready, Set, page 10.) You can do an abbreviated loop through the neighbourhood by taking a right off Marine onto the clearly marked Taylor Way, then just past the Upper Levels intersection veer right onto Stevens. You are now circling the **Capilano Golf and Country Club,** an integral part of the 50-year-old community plan. As you turn quite sharply around the north corner of the golf course watch for Kenwood Rd. and take it right. Don't take its first right-hand branch onto Groveland but the next, very near one onto Eyremont Dr. By now you have noticed the tendency toward low-slung, cliff-hugging cedar bungalows boasting exquisite landscaping and even more exquisite views of Vancouver, the Straight of Georgia to the west, Howe Sound to the northwest and the mountains of northern Washington to the south.

A couple of real Eyremont beauties, both inspired by Japanese aesthetics, are on the 1100 block. Renowned architect Ron Thom designed the ultra-modern cedar-and-glass home at 1143, and builder Robert Lewis constructed his own home at 1124 with fine woodwork and roof contours more directly borrowed from Japanese architecture. Take the next left, Crestwell, which soon turns into Chartwell and winds back downhill to the Upper Levels Highway. Go right (west) to **Horseshoe Bay,** a 10-minute drive. Watch for the Horseshoe Bay/B.C. Ferries turnoff veering left; the Upper Levels at that point continues northward as Highway 99 to Squamish and Whistler.

At this point a number of touring options are open to you. You can call it a day—but not before sampling the home brewed Bay Ale at **The Troller Pub** (6422 Bay, 921-7616). One bottle, please, if you're driving. If you want a pastoral adventure, take the Horseshoe Bay ferry to **Bowen Island,** a picturesque little piece of cottage country just 20-minutes from the mainland. You can drive around the tiny island, hike up the heavily wooded hills for better views (trails are well marked) or snuggle up for an hour or two at Bowen's one restaurant, **The Snuggler** (947-2423), just up the road from the ferry. Boats leave almost hourly, and charge $8.45 for car and driver, round trip.

A slightly longer ferry ride takes you from Horseshoe Bay clear across the mouth of Howe Sound to **Langdale,** southernmost point of the ruggedly scenic Sunshine Coast. Sparsley populated in the winter but packed with camping tourists in summer, I think this colourful bit of coastline warrants a visit any time of year. At the very least, stop in **Gibsons,** just a few km. from the ferry landing at Langdale. Besides being a charming fishing town, it holds interest to CBC-TV watchers as the cuter-than-quaint setting of "The Beachcombers"—Molly's Reach and all. Star Bruno Gerussi has a home up in the hills.

You can relax in one of the Gower Point Road cafes before returning, or keep driving north along Highway 101 to the slightly larger town of Sechelt, which has slightly more sophisticated eating places, about 20 minutes up the Sunshine Coast. Right on the highway, in a lovely old white house across from the harbour just as you enter Sechelt, is **Casa Martinez** (885-2911) where you can get a killer paella.

The Langdale Ferry takes about 45 minutes, leaves every two to three hours and costs $16.95 for car and driver, round trip. During the summer and holiday weekends it is a good idea to call B.C. Ferries (669-1211) for advice on which are the least congested sailings.

For a return drive from Horseshoe Bay to Vancouver,

try the coast-hugging Marine Drive instead of the Upper Levels Highway. It is a slower, more scenic route along the lower but far from lowly residential neighbourhoods. Again, the dominant look is rambling, modernistic cedar-and-skylight bungalows with rock gardens and shrubbery that make the most of this truly exceptional strip of real estate. Along the way you'll see a sign to Lighthouse Park, and if you have on your sou'wester and your rubber-tread shoes you might want to clamber onto the rocks for a quiet seaward contemplation. From there Marine takes you back through a pretty shopping area to the clearly marked ramp onto the Lions Gate Bridge.

Take a Powder:

Where Rain Turns White

Between November and March, rain in the city generally means snow in the mountains, and that's good enough reason to drop everything and drive on up. Here are a few of your choices, most of them less than an hour from downtown.

Grouse Mountain

This is the most easily accessible ski area to the city, and the easiest to see from any starting point—providing the shaved strip of alpine that runs down Grouse's face isn't obscured by cloud. At night, the lights of Grouse have become a towering landmark on scale with the great Corcovado cross of Rio de Janeiro.

The "Superskyride" tram to the alpine base is probably the classic tourist experience in Vancouver, summer or winter. Of course, on cloudy days it is only worthwhile if you have skiing or hiking in mind. The skyride loads from a massive parking lot 13 km. from downtown (Lions Gate Bridge, right on Marine Dr. East, left on Capilano Rd.). Grouse Mountain (snow report, 986-6262; other information, 984-0661) offers day and magnificent night skiing November through April; four double lifts, two T-bars and three rope tows service a good variety of runs with 300-metre drop; and lessons, rentals and dining at the upper skyride station are also available.

Cypress Bowl

This is a popular family mountain, also 13 km. from downtown but on the West Vancouver side. (Hwy. 1 toward Horseshoe Bay, turn right at Cypress Access Rd.) From early December through March (depending on snow) Cypress (ski report, 922-0176; other details,

929-3911) offers eight beginner, intermediate and advanced runs over 358 metres vertical; two chairs and one double tow; 30 km. of well marked, groomed cross-country trails; equipment rentals and maps; a cafeteria at the bowl; and a lodge with 11 guest rooms six km. away.

Seymour Mountain

Mt. Seymour Provincial Park (details, 683-3421) is 15 km. northeast of downtown, lying between North Vancouver and the charming community of Deep Cove. (Fastest route is via Second Narrows Bridge to Keith Rd., and onto the Mt. Seymour Parkway.) Once in the park you snake up the mountain for another 13 km. to the alpine base level. If the clouds lift even momentarily, you will be treated to one of the great Vancouver vistas—from Indian Arm on the east to the Gulf Islands and San Juans on the west. Available are day and night skiing from early December to early May on a 204-metre drop, chiefly beginner and intermediate runs; two chairlifts and four rope tows; fine cross-country trails and facilities; and a cafeteria in the day lodge.

Whistler/Blackcomb Mountains

These sister resorts nestled in the Coast Mountains (Garibaldi Park) 120 km. north of Vancouver are British Columbia's claim to world-class skiing. (Whistler, 112-932-5528; Blackcomb, 112-932-3141; snow reports, 687-6761/687-7507). Even if you don't ski, you will find the drive along Howe Sound and inland through Squamish to the charming ski village to be a day trip well worth the time and gas. Developers are trying hard to make Whistler/Blackcomb a year-round destination, with hiking trails, golf, tennis, windsurfing on Alta Lake and numerous fine eateries and watering holes. But summer is sleepy compared with ski season, late November to early May.

The two resorts sell a combination ski pass, but if you are just up for the day you won't have time to give both mountains a go. It is a short day (9 a.m. to 3:30 p.m.) and the runs are extremely long—many of them over 1,000 metres. So choose your mountain: Whistler is the old-time favourite, boasting the greatest vertical drop in North American (1,305 metres) plus a terrific variety of services; Blackcomb is the recent upstart, presenting stiff competition with what many believe is a superior fall-line and many more intermediate runs. You can't lose either way.

Hemlock Valley

At this early stage of Hemlock's development, it mainly has snow going for it—lots and lots of powder. Located 125 km. east of Vancouver on Hwy. 7, Hemlock (112-525-1944) takes advantage of Interior B.C. snowfalls by offering wide-open bowl skiing, very well serviced with chairs. (Much shorter lineups here on weekends than at most other resorts.) It includes a vertical drop of 350 metres in the alpine area; six km. of trails in cross country; and good accommodations, food, rentals, lessons.

Manning Park

It's a fair drive to the Gibson Pass ski area (112-926-6071) at Manning (230 km. east of Vancouver on Hwy. 3), but if the snow is thin and mushy at the coastal resorts and you're in a desperate mood to ski, the three hours may not seem excessive. From December to April you are guaranteed deep powdery snow at this park high up in the Cascade Mountains. Manning is especially renowned for its cross-country trails—some 170 km. of them, all levels. Downhill is pretty well no-frills, no-nonsense skiing for the whole family. Rates tend to be cheaper than most other resorts. Rentals and lessons are available for both.

PUBS & CLUBS

The High Life

There is only one thing more fickle than the top 10 records on AM radio—the top 10 nightclubs in Vancouver, so you will have to forgive me if a dazzling new club has appeared to top the list since we went to press. If you want to find out about it, just go to any of these hot spots and tune in for word-of-mouth:

Confetti (1255 West Pender, 681-5201) is the new wave in discos—funky fifties decor (Superman mannequin in a phone booth, front end of a '53 Cadillac poking through a wall) plus Euro-pop music, light show, rock videos and two dance floors packed with a moneyed, soft-punk crowd. Restaurateur Bud Kanke of The Cannery and Mulvaney's made Confetti rise from the ashes of his old Viva! club when the supply of middle-aged, Gucci-clad disco bunnies dried up. If you can take the "Hi, grandpa" looks that anyone over 25 gets here, you're guaranteed a colourful evening. Pizza and burgers served. Cover $2. Open 8 to 2.

Richard's on Richards (1036 Richards, 687-6794) is where three-piece suiters peel down to two and hustle secretaries who have traded in their shirtwaists and sensible shoes for clingy silk and spandex. It's the classiest meet market in town, with lots of brass and stained glass and a gorgeous bar installed where the stage of this lovely old theatre used to be. Bands play top 40 AOR (adult-oriented rock) and on weekends people line up clear down Richards St. to get down and boogie. $4 cover on weekends. 7 to 2.

Systems (350 Richards, 687-5007) is an enormous, expensive, high-tech temple dedicated to new-age disco dancing. A medium-young, slightly preppy crowd flocks here for a turn on the 1,800-square-foot hardwood dance floor. Hundreds of feet of neon carve the space into tripped-out geometry, and a rotating laser sends sheets of light slicing through the room to the rock pulse. Don't go to mingle (high-tech chrome furnishings are not designed for a snuggle-up conversation). Go to dance. $3 Monday through Thursday, $5 weekends. 8 to 2.

Pelican Bay (1253 Johnston, 683-7535) is for serious mingling. The crowd at this Granville Island Hotel disco/lounge is the chronic 29-year-old variety—impeccably dressed, just a hint of punk-chic, cynical about love, and devoted to wine. By day Pelican Bay is a trendy restaurant (see page 112) so it doesn't clear a dance space until 10 p.m. at which time the joint is always packed to the celadon green rafters. Your best bet is to have dinner and stay for the night. No cover. 10 to 1:30.

The Railway Club (579 Beatty, 681-1625) is described by my high-living writer friend Les Wiseman as "the least pretentious good nightclub in town." About 3,500 people (loggers, poets, punks and stock brokers) pay $10 a year to be members of this club that used to cater to railroad line supervisors. You can get in without membership (members pay $1 cover on weekends, you pay $3) but you don't get all the perks, like a key to let yourself in during the afternoon for a secret lounge retreat. Dancing is possible though not popular (space is limited) but the listening is serious thanks to a daring program of original music by some of Vancouver's most interesting new bands—from rockabilly to reggae. Noon to 2 a.m.

Luv-A-Fair (1275 Seymour, 685-3288) is where you go if you either want to be thoroughly outrageous or get an eyeful of outrageousness. Formerly a gay disco, the club now attracts an even mix of high-fashion hairdressers, safety-pinned punkers, full-out drag queens and wide-eyed gawkers. It has one of the hottest dance floors in town, and one of the best sound systems pumping out imported English/German new-wave music against a backdrop of rock videos. Occasional live concerts draw huge crowds, but normally you can squeeze in without lining up. $3 cover on weekends. Open 9 to 2.

One of the few old faithful clubs is Humphrey Killam's **The Ankor** (99 Powell, 669-4022) in Gastown, featuring a no surprises line-up of the best local rhythm 'n blues bands. No matter what's happening in the trendier places, first-rate musicians like Jim Byrnes and Al Foreman will pack this joint every time they play it. Good dancing on the main floor, good watching on the balcony. $2 cover. 8 to 2.

The current watering hole for students is **Darby D. Dawes,** (2001 Macdonald, 731-0617) a neighbourhood pub in Kits with a great snack menu (nachos, salmon rolls, pasta) and cozy English pub atmosphere. There's a jazz pianist at lunch and a good, mixed line-up of rock bands Thursday through Saturday evenings. The only problem is the "pub" license which requires it to close at 11 p.m. No cover.

Here are a couple of quiet ones: **Plazazz** (1999 Marine, North Van, 984-0611) has a silly name, but this show lounge in North Vancouver's International Plaza Hotel compensates with a seriously good program of live jazz. Oscar Peterson, Ella Fitzgerald, Tonny Bennett and contemporary artists like The Nylons have performed in this intimate 250-seat lounge. (Compared to the Queen Elizabeth Theatre where you'd normally see acts like these, Plazazz is virtually one-on-one.) Prices vary widely. Tickets at VTC/CBO outlets. Two shows nightly, 8 and 10:30 Monday through Saturday.

And quieter still, there's **Bridges** (1696 Duranleau, 687-4400)—the Granville Island restaurant and wine bistro where light jazz and classical music stays deep in the background where it belongs on those important tete-a-tete nights. Expensively designed in the street-side Paris bistro style and staffed by sexy young waiters and lithe mini-skirted waitresses, it's hard to decide whether to fix your gaze inside or out through the picture windows overlooking False Creek. The wine list is tasteful and long, with the added benefit of a great many carafe and by-the-glass choices. Noon to 12:30 a.m. daily.

The Simple Life

Serious lounge lizards know that it's easier to find a hot nightclub than it is to find a plain, decent bar to call your own. I don't pretend to know your taste in draft or decor, but I would like to share some favourites of mine and my no-nonsense drinking buddies.

But first, for the benefit of visitors, a word about the beers of choice in these parts. While our Eastern Canadian drinking friends stick to their strong ales and our southern neighbours sip their weak stuff, British Columbians generally prefer lagers like Molson's Canadian—the standard five percent alcohol in a light-bodied beer. Pilseners are also popular here (same alcohol level, stronger hops taste) with Labatt's Blue and the new upstart Kokanee topping the polls. Health-minded guzzlers stick to Iron Horse which has no additives. And those who need an extra kick order malt liquors (6.5 percent) like O'Keefe's Extra Old Stock or Columbia Extra. The current bargain beer is simply called Beer, adorned with plain brown label and sold in bulk at government liquor stores in a matching carton.

On to the bars: **The Sylvia** (1154 Gilford, 681-9321) has for years been the only thoroughly unpretentious English Bay lounge. We'll have to reserve judgement on it at present though; renovations were about to begin as this book went to press and you never know what might rise out of the rubble. Let's hope the same formula will endure—the two-dollar scotch and the million-dollar view. Monday to Thursday 4 to midnight, weekends 11 to 1.

Downstairs in the Georgia Hotel, the **King George V Pub** (801 West Georgia, 682-5566) has a well-aged British tavern decor with a clientele to match. Dark Duffy draft is on tap, shepherd's pie and cornish pastries are always on the lunch menu, and weekend entertainment leans toward sing-alongs by the likes of kilted Robbie Stuart and his Publicans. A warm and friendly place. 11:30 a.m. to 1 a.m.

Chaser's Lounge at the Fraser Arms Hotel (1450 South West Marine, 261-7277) is a favourite sports-watching bar, with a 15-foot video screen taking centre stage whenever there is a major event. On other nights it shows rock videos, with the exception of Tuesdays when the screen is upstaged entirely by live stand-up comedians. Drinking is serious here (beer, highballs) but if you get peckish you can grab a snack in the Milltown pub next door or in the hotel coffee shop. Don't get too serious about the booze, though. You can be sure the bouncers are in better shape than you are. (The bouncer list at one time included sports heavyweights like B.C. Lions player Brent Racette and brother Gordy, the boxer.) Open 8:30 to 2.

The "urban cowboy" trend came and went, but at least one city bar remained plain ol' country before, during and after—the **American Hotel** (928 Main St., 681-5839). Mind you, this is not the kind of 10-gallon country bar you'd find in Surrey or Langley. The American is a raunchy country-rock hangout, featuring strippers by day and live bands at night. It draws a mixed crowd—downtown downers, uptown business people, tough guys in leather-and-studs and young kids in jeans and runners. It can get a tad hostile when the bikers are home from a run, but usually the American is a regular bar to get pie-eyed and blow off a little steam. Don't go alone. 11 to 1:30.

P.T.'s, the bar at the Lone Star Hotel (412 Carrall, 681-5948), is a bustling, noisy place filled with people playing pool, ping pong, darts, fooze ball and Pac Man, watching the big-screen TV or listening to Paul (P.T.) Tyer's run-on ruminations about life in general. Lone Star is always on tap, Tyer is always on, and if you're there on a Tuesday evening you can count on some red hot competition in the table tennis tourneys. The Lone Star dates back to 1906 and so does a lot of the decor, but Tyer claims the toilets are so clean you could roll around on the floor in there and come up smellin' like roses. We didn't take him up on it, but yes, it does look pretty decent. 11:30 to 1:30 a.m.

Molly Hogan's Pub (Knight and 41st, phone unlisted) is one of those mellow neighbourhood bars that regulars like to keep all to themselves. Sorry fellas. This place is so warm and inviting I just couldn't leave it out. Three loggers-turned-businessmen are behind Molly Hogan's and they've filled the place with logging paraphernalia, rough-hewn wood furnishings and hearty cookhouse-style food—hoganburgers, chili, baron of beef...The crowd is a friendly mix of east end working folk, college kids and the odd sports celebrity (B.C. Lions player Larry Crawford is a regular). Toby is on tap, mellow music is on tape during the day and top 40 rock at night. Open 11 to 11.

The After Life

A few years ago the best recommendation I could have made to you on where to cool down after a heated night or heat up after a mellow one would be to invite the gang back to your place. Fortunately, the late-late scene is flourishing these days. You can save your carpets and your liqueur stock by wiling away the wee hours in one of these sleepless haunts:

Basin St. (163 East Hastings, 681-2927) wins hands down for atmosphere. This is the east-side Vancouver version of Old Montreal—a dimly lit, smoky little jazz club dedicated to top-flight live music and die-hard insomniacs. The best local musicians come here to jam the night away, urged on by a lot of visiting musicians who wind up here after they've finished their straight sets in uptown hotel lounges. It serves coffee and snacks. Cover $2 for members (membership is $10 a year), $5 for guests. Open Friday and Saturday, 1:30 a.m. to 5:30.

Paradise Club (1251 Howe, 682-4561) is as hot as Basin St. is mellow. The infamous "Robin," formerly DJ of the ultra-chic gay disco Gandy Dancer, flips the progressive rock discs here and attracts a young, seriously trendy crowd seven nights a week. Don't let the pretty, peach-coloured courtyard decor fool you. The Paradise Club rocks hard. The dance floor is often jammed right up to the 5 a.m. closing. If you still have the faculty of sight, watch for rock celebrities filtering in after their concert gigs (David Bowie and band were sighted recently). Cover $3 before midnight, $5 after, $3 on Sundays. Open 10 p.m. to 5 a.m. Monday to Saturday, 10 to 2 Sundays.

The **Hot Jazz Society** (36 East Broadway, 873-4131) offers Dixieland and swing jazz bands and lots of dancing for the jive set. This is the kind of friendly, no-airs place where you could do jumping jacks on the dance floor and it would be okay—as long as you're in time. There's a full bar and light snacks. This is really a society—memberships sold at the door for a nominal price. Open Tuesday through Saturday, 8:30 on. (No fixed closing.)

The Montgomery Cafe (433 West Pender, 685-5524, see also page 114) is the cool spot to wind down Friday and Saturday nights after a performance-art show at the Unit Pitt Gallery. If you can take the heady mix of new wave musicians getting unwired, street-smart artists sharing their vision with punk poets and hairstylists of the New Romantic persuasion soaking it all in, you will undoubtedly enjoy the animation of the place. Formerly the Stork Club Restaurant, circa 1952, the Montgomery has integrated new touches like neon wall art and an espresso machine into the old cafe fixtures—S-shaped counter, old soda fountain, backroom booths looking in on the greasy-chips kitchen. Wine, beer and surprisingly decent light meals. Progressive music on tape. 11 a.m. to midnight Monday to Thursday, to 4 a.m. Friday and Saturday.

If you're one of those normal people with an after life that starts around 11:30 p.m. when the movie gets out, flip ahead to pages 116 & 117 for some leads on "Coffee Plus" destinations like **Cheesecake Etc., L'Espresso di Zanetta** and **Ciao,** or to page 115 where you will find the delightful **Binky's Oyster Bar,** or to page 112 for one of my personal favourites—**Bridges.**

BINKY'S
OYSTER BAR
& RESTAURANT

ALL DAY DINING

Lingering Over Lunch

I'm calling it lunch for brevity, but what we're really talking about here is any meal of substance that crosses the lips before suppertime. For a light snack and in-between cuppa, look to the "Cafe Society" section. For dinner, keep on reading. The chief criteria for all these sections are quality of food plus staying appeal—a factor of crucial importance to the rainy-day diner in particular. Even if the food is terrific you are not going to get value out of a place that serves in a big hurry and sends you flying back out the revolving doors into the rain-slicked streets. Here are the top-ranking places in my survey, for your lingering pleasure:

Best Brunches

Rain or shine, the most enchanted brunch spot in town is **The Teahouse Restaurant** in Stanley Park (Ferguson Point, 669-3281). If you are falling in love, this place will tie the knot. You must make a reservation for the Saturday and Sunday brunches (ask for a conservatory table where you will be certain you're a continent away in an English country garden), serving 10:30 a.m. to 2:30. The food is not great—upper-crust English with a bland French influence—but you can't go far wrong with quiche and omelette choices.

The best brunch-with-view places are on Granville Island: Upstairs at **Bridges** (1650 Duranleau, 687-4400) you are treated to one of the city's most creative brunch menus in a highly sophisticated and comfortable dining room surrounded by picture windows looking over the False Creek marinas to the downtown skyline and North Shore mountains. Are you ready for their Green Eggs & Ham? (Poached eggs, crab and ham on a croissant with broccoli and spinach sauce.) Served 10 to 4. **Pelican Bay** at the Granville Island Hotel (1253 Johnston, 683-7373) is where the beautiful people linger, but it may be a bit rich for your tastes. Brunch is closer to lunch here, with entrees like the wonderfully tender Polynesian-style Chicken Saute, served 11-3.

Also famous for brunch-with-view is West Vancouver's **Salmon House on the Hill** (2229 Folkstone Way, near the 21st St. exit on Upper Levels Hwy., 926-3212) where you get an amazing view of Vancouver across Burrard Inlet—that is, if you can see over the mountain of food on your plate. Specialty is the alderwood-smoked salmon.

Reservations are not accepted and brunch is very popular so be prepared to wait in the lounge-with-view where champagne-and-orange-juice are served.

One goes to **Mark James** (2486 Bayswater, 734-1325) for the food. The view here is limited to the lovely skylit interior and beautiful people, and the menu is quite simple but delicious—omelettes, croissants, fresh-squeezed juices and great coffee.

Dim sum is the best way to make brunch stretch out into a full afternoon. The best Chinese restaurants are no longer in Chinatown: The **Pink Pearl** (1132 East Hastings, 253-4316) is a large, no-nonsense family restaurant with an enormously popular Cantonese-style dim sum. A bit fancier is **Flamingo House** (7510 Cambie, 325-4511) specializing in fresh fish and seafood, or the quite westernized **Peninsula** (604 West Broadway, 872-1271) featuring some 40 gourmet items served from the classic rolling carts.

Food critic and restaurateur James Barber favours the Szechuan delicacies at **Yang's** (4186 Main, 873-2116) where spicy, noodle-based dishes make an excellent brunch for the adventurous. Mom and Pop Yang do a magic show of noodle-making Saturday at noon.

Lunch: Basic

You can get a decent BLT sandwich anywhere, but where can you dive into a great bowl of matzo ball soup? **The Triangle** (302 West Cordova, 684-2712) is a little-known Jewish cafe that has been hiding at this downtown corner for 21 years, serving soul-warming soups and smoked meat sandwiches to a local clientele that prefers to keep it a secret. It's so small you can hear all about what Sidney ("the chef") and Renee ("manager") Gerundfeld watched last night on TV. They're only open 7 to 4, perfect for lunch with the kids because no one minds a little noise and they have perch seats for little ones plus real kidfood on the menu—kosher weiners and beans, grilled cheese sandwich with peach quarter, that kind of stuff.

Nearby is another well-kept secret, but this one among a young and trendy crowd. The **Montgomery Cafe** (433 West Pender, 685-5524) is "your classic '80s rock-n-roll cafe" according to new-wave fashion consultant Robynne Ranft who knows. Owner/designer David Birdsall did an "Eisenhower modern" makeover of the 30-year-old coffee shop, putting in fake pony-hide banquettes and touches of neon. It serves cheap, wholesome diner-style food including $1.99 breakfast all day.

No-frills fish fanciers have recently discovered a new alternative to **The Only,** the greasy spoon at 20 East Hastings where you get it very fresh, very plain, very cheap. **Marine View Cafe** is the new buzz (975 Centennial Pier, 253-0616) and if you manage to find this fisherman's lunch counter down near B.C. Sugar, you will know why the rumour is spreading. Ruby Gurney and her girls serve fish and seafood so fresh you can almost see it wiggle. Good helpings of fried sole, halibut and other fresh catch, deep-fried clam strips and towering crab/shrimp sandwiches go for $3.50 to $5. Open 7 to 2. Get there by taking the Heatly overpass north from Powell, veer right past Ballantyne Pier and go into the parking lot just west of the two-storey red brick CN building.

Lunch: Posh

The latest "in" spot downtown is **Binky's Oyster Bar** (784 Thurlow, 681-7073) where you can slurp golden mantles or bluepoints in the front cafe or settle in for a more serious meal of oyster stew or fresh fish in the back restaurant. Reigning queen of the local literati Celia Duthie (Duthie Books, Manhattan Books, M.C. Duthie Gallery) is behind this swishy joint, and her impeccable taste both on the menu and in the magazine rack is winning her a faithful coterie of Oyster Barflies.

The ultra-rich and ultra-fussy flock to Barbara Gordon's **La Cachette** in Kerrisdale (2036 West 41st, 266-0824) where the exquisitely tasteful nouvelle cuisine menu is only matched by the presentation. You can easily overdose from the elaborate and very expensive five-course dinners. My preference here is lunch—quite simple but absolutely perfect. Herbs are always fresh, eggs always from range chickens, meats perfectly aged or fresh-cured. One of the best wine lists in town.

If you want hearty but not heavy, you can't beat a bistro for lunch. My favourite is **Le Bistro** (747 Thurlow, 681-3818)—a crowded, cozy place where you can fill up on the baked onion soup, excellent baguette and decent house wine for under $10. The huge salad nicoise is the businesswomen's favourite, $6. You can lunch more elegantly on fish, duck or rabbit pates at **Le Bistro La Palette** (774 Denman, 681-6844) where chef Mitsui Fujikawa combines the best of Japanese and French cuisine to arrive at the most colourful and artistic presentations I have ever seen. (Hence the name.) They also taste good.

If you are in Gastown and have some time to wile away, head for **The Restaurant at Le Magasin** (332 Water, 687-1029) where people who have patience are rewarded with the tastiest souffles in town. In fact, these may well be the only real souffles in town because most restaurants don't figure people will wait while they prepare them properly, from scratch. They warn you at Le Magasin that it will take half an hour (actually, it can take 45 minutes) which works out just fine if you have a loose schedule and a decent wine budget. Choices include gruyere, crab & shrimp, apple & calvados, hazlenut...$7 with salad.

Cafe Society

Vancouver's historic roots may be in England, but one quick glance at the cafe scene will tell you how much our city is flavoured by Europe these days. Okay, there are a few places that still serve high tea, but by and large your choices range from Italian espresso and ice cream through stuffed croissants, chocolate truffle and Perrier. Below, the cream of the cafes:

Coffee Plus

Serious sippers will tell you the best espresso is in Little Italy, but I'm not so sure. I live in Kitsilano, surrounded by students who could never make it through college without caffeine, and a number of excellent coffee bars have sprung up along West 4th catering to their around-the-clock needs. The neighbourhood favourite is **El Cerrito** (1938 West 4th, 732-3114), run by Lorne Berkan who started the whole tradition in Kits with his **Boca Bar** (3525 West 4th, 731-8522) 12 years ago. El Cerrito doesn't have the Boca's great newspaper rack, but it does have a more attractive and varied menu including inexpensive all-day breakfasts of espresso-steamed eggs, thick slabs of ham, Mexican corn bread or croissants. All the coffees are good. Only problem is, this place is so laid back you might have to wake up a waiter to get service.

The favourite night-time haunt of students and newly affluent ex-hippies is **Cheesecake Etc.** (2141 Granville, 734-7704) where the mood is mellow, the conversation is good, the coffees and herbal teas tastefully prepared and the cheesecake (especially chocolate) absolutely delicious in the light, melt-in-your-mouth, West Coast style. Owner Michael Sims is not going to get famous for his piano playing (he entertains whenever the spirit moves him) but he and his place are so endearing that he always gets a warm round of applause. There is an arts/entertainment review board at the front for self-professed critics—always good for a hoot.

I really don't have to direct you to the espresso bars in Little Italy—just go to Commercial Drive and you'll find more than a dozen steamy little joints between Venables and East 2nd. (See page 23 for details on a few of them.) My friend Susan Mendelson, cookbook author and partner in the catering shop The Lazy Gourmet, steered me into the **Pofi Bar** (1308 Commercial, 253-5416) for the best and cheapest Hazelnut gelati in town, and later into **Continental Billiards** (1150 Commercial, 255-5626) where it takes a bit of courage for an unescorted woman to saunter up to the bar and order cappuccino, but it's definitely worth it.

Dominic Bombara started the Italian ice cream craze in Vancouver 15 years ago, and his gelati/espresso bar

Venezia (5752 Victory, 327-8614) is still a favourite among purists. But for the truly decadent, **Ping Pong** is the current name in Italian ice cream. It's now at three locations as well as in grocery stores and on dessert menus all over town, but that doesn't detract from the delightful indulgence of tucking into the Ice Cream Bomb (hazelnut, chocolate, zabaglione and amaretto topped with fresh fruit and whipped cream, $3.60) at the original Neo-Deco parlor on Robson (1129, 683-5341). Great coffees too.

No matter where you're shopping, you are never far from a caffeine fix. In the downtown core: **L'Espresso di Zanatta** (609 Robson, 681-3614) is slightly chic, slightly funky—very European; **Ciao** (1074 Denman, 682-0112) has the best cappuccino and gateaux in the West End; **Le Chocolat Belge Daniel** (2260 West 41st, 263-2335) is a cozy Kerrisdale truffle-and-espresso parlor that even smells deliciously expensive—$24 a kilo for Daniel Poncelet's wonderful chocolates.

Tea, High & Low

You have to search high and low for proper 4 p.m. English tea in this city; if you're dying for the real thing, a day trip to Victoria for **Tea at The Empress** is your only recourse. Restaurant critic James Barber who relishes the soothing experience of afternoon tea ("less alcoholic than lunch, less demanding than dinner, less scandalous than a bar") says his all-time favourite is the **Yip Hong Yuen Bakery** (288 East Pender, 683-4621) which serves the tasty black Pu Erh tea plus a huge selection of moon cakes, sugary buns and pastries.

But if you want the true atmosphere of high tea and are willing to compromise on the menu, the most elegant tea in town is served in the Garden Lounge at **The Four Seasons Hotel** (791 West Georgia, 689-9333) where there is a choice of six teas, pricey but good open-face sandwiches and dessert.

The downtown pastry shops come closer to the right menu (a proper selection of nibblies rolled around on carts) but then you often sacrifice atmosphere. Best pastries are certainly at the **Bon Ton** (874 Granville, 681-3058) but you have to put up with the crush of people in line for their take-out baking plus the insufferably poky service. More inviting is **The Danish Tea Room** (1068 Robson, 683-3732) where you might easily be confused by the name and the curry dishes on the menu. Relax, this is an English-style tea room run by Ismailis from Tanzania, which is a far cry from Regent Street but a solid part of the Old Empire nevertheless. Choose from 12 teas, tasty pastries and tortes, and an eclectic menu of sandwiches, samosas and curries.

A definitely West Coast tea is served at **Isadora's** on Granville Island (1540 Old Bridge, 681-8816) where the tea is unremarkable but the scones and muffins could easily take your right through supper. Seniors get the best shake here—high tea complete for $1.65.

Dwelling Over Dinner

On rainy nights you don't just want to dine, you want to dwell over your food. In the interest of endurance eating, I have selected a handful of restaurants which include some of Vancouver's finest but which, more importantly, offer a variety of ways to wile away the evening hours around the table.

It won't take you a moment to notice my bias in favour of ethnic restaurants. That is not only because I was weaned on beet borscht and chopped herring. It's also because in my quest for places to dwell over dinner I have discovered that people in ethnic restaurants do it the best. They really know how to kick back and have a good time around the table. They leave their soggy spirits and shoes at the door, and slip away to another country for the night—any country! Perhaps if you come from Toronto or New York you will take it for granted, but most people I know are knocked off their feet by the ethnic variety of Vancouver's restaurants. The Indonesian rice tables, Spanish tapas bars, Japanese tatamis and Indian tandoori houses I mention below are just a start.

Divine Nibbling

Nowhere can you find more soothing shelter from a rainy night than in your own private tatami suite in a Japanese restaurant. **Kamei Sushi** (811 Thurlow, 684-4823) is the current choice, famous for its makunouchi—the "Bullet Train Special" based on the box lunch served passengers travelling between Tokyo and Osaka. There is a sampling in it of Kamei's specialties, including excellent marinated vegetables and some simple sushi for novices. Off the beaten track but highly respected by connoisseurs is **Jinya** (657 West Broadway, 873-5040) where sushi chef Tojo works magic with raw abalone, geoduck and other exotica from the sea. Everything, including the old favourites like salmon teriyaki and prawns tempura, are prepared and presented to perfection, served crackling hot by charming waitresses.

Too many Chinese restaurants hurl the food at you so quickly that it's all you can do to make your dinner last an hour. (Ever tried dwelling over a fortune cookie?) There are exceptions: **Flamingo House** (7510 Cambie, 325-4511) is my choice for fine Chinese dining. There are surprising appetizers, like lettuce and spiced beef roll-ups, crispy chicken skins with prawn chips and a wonderfully sensuous winter melon soup, plus a great variety of fresh-from-the-tank fish and seafood entrees.

For a slight deviation in Oriental fare and a great conversation starter, try the Indonesian rice table at **Taksangka** (3916 Main, 876-0121). A dozen different meat, vegetable and condiment dishes are spread around the giant rice bowl for a hearty communal meal. There are hints of India, China and the Middle East here, all delicately seasoned for a very tasty mix.

Fondue is a meal that lasts and lasts. The classic Swiss style is served at **Chez Beat** (1127 West Broadway, 734-2735) where the raclette (gruyere and emmenthaler cheese) is more interesting than the meat fondues. An interesting twist is the fondue-like Korean style of cooking your own lean strips of beef on a grill in the centre of your table at **The New Seoul** (1682 East Broadway, 872-1922 or 845 East Hastings, 255-8625).

If you have a Western palate you have no choice but to linger over your curry, with plenty of cold beer and chapattis to quell the flames. Indian food has risen to the gourmet ranks in Vancouver with the opening of two superb restaurants, both specializing in the tandoori-style barbecued meats and breads of the Punjab. The newest is **Bombay Palace** (1050 West Pender, 683-6551), an elegant, quiet downtown spot to savour rich "Butter Chicken" or spiced meats that arrive at your table still sizzling from the coal grill. The **Raga** (1177 West Broadway, 733-1127) is a livelier place, often so crowded you won't get in without a reservation. You can easily make a whole meal out of the stuffed roti breads—spicy but not too hot.

You'll find curry with a difference at **Kilimanjaro** (308 Water, 681-9913) where Indian and African fare is blended in a unique and delicious manner. Beef kabobs and lamb grilled the Arabic way share the menu with Indian curries and African specialties like the mixture of plantains, peanuts and beef called "matoke nyama." Ask the waiter for advice on combining these dishes, and order a little at a time for a long and decadent Eastern feast.

Let me finish up by letting you in on the very best way to brighten up even the darkest, dreariest nights of winter—Spanish tapas. The Spanish understand better than anyone how food goes down best: delicately spiced, charcoal grilled in tasty little bits, and washed down slowly over several hours of easy conversation, lively music and plenty of earthy wine.

Mark Winrob's **Las Tapas** has popularized the Spanish style of elegant "snack bar" dining. There are now locations in Vancouver, North Vancouver and Richmond, but I prefer the original Las Tapas (760 Cambie, 669-1624) for atmosphere—the crackling fireplace on cold evenings; the buzz of activity along the tapas and wine bar; the flamenco troupe that struts through regularly on weekends. Every dish is offered in three sizes, which means you can do a lot of sampling and reordering if you stick with the small ones. The marinated squid, sauteed chicken livers, grilled lamb and breaded zucchini are dependably tasty. (One warning: Tell your waiter in advance to bring everything steaming hot.)

Simply Divine

Rainy or not, there are a few restaurants that you simply mustn't miss if you have the time and money to indulge yourself in food and service fit for royalty. Appetizers at the restaurants below generally cost $6 to $10, entrees up to $26 (in 1984 dollars). So bring your American Express gold card, and leave your scruples at the door.

The **William Tell** has been at the top of many Vancouver gourmands' dining lists for years and although the location and the menu have changed recently I can report that this is still a wonderful place to indulge the palate. Owner Erwin Doebeli and his internationally acclaimed chef Kurt Kuhn have moved the whole operation from the rather stuffy old restaurant at 765 Beatty down the street into the airy new Georgian Court hotel (722 Beatty, 688-3504). The menu has also moved in the direction of clean and light, dispensing with the remnants of traditional Swiss cuisine (the fondues) and adding a variety of nouvelle cuisine items. But the William Tell is still a great place to take traditionalists—they can dig into their chateaubriand while you savour an appetizer of pheasant parfait with goose liver and an entree of squab in puff pastry with cabbage and truffles.

Le Pavillon at The Four Seasons (791 West Georgia, 689-9333) has undergone a more serious change this year with the loss of executive chef Michel Clavelin, the eccentric Frenchman who elevated this establishment from the ranks of fine hotel dining to Vancouver's premiere French restaurant. I am pleased to report that his successor Rudi Mack has maintained the same impeccable standards. This is old-style French dining, where service (dignified, doting) is at least as important as the food. There is something about being treated so royally that psychs you into believing the food is magnificent. Well, it's pretty damn good here, psych or no.

For the finest northern Italian food, try any of Umberto Menghi's five restaurants. It is unusual for an empire builder like the charismatic Mr. Menghi to keep the standards high as his sphere of influence grows, but the undying popularity of Umberto's places among some of this town's most discriminating diners attests to his success. **Il Giardino** (1382 Hornby, 669-2422) features game as well as Italian classics from pasta through veal bucco, served up in a casually elegant country garden setting; **La Cantina** (1376 Hornby, 687-6621) specializes in fresh fish and seafood dishes while the original **Umberto's** right next door (687-6316) serves the haut cuisine of Florence—saucy and rich; **Il Palazzo** (432 Richards, 687-3733) is a divinely decadent version of Umberto's, surrounding the Florentine food with lavish Renaissance decor; **Al Porto** (321 Water, 683-8376) is a rambling, airy trattoria with no pretension but simply great antipasto, pasta and meat/fish/chicken entrees. Il Giardino and Al Porto are open for lunch as well as dinner.

An Italian alternative: when **Massimo** (1355 Hornby, 688-1916) opened directly across the street from Umberto's mini-empire a few years ago a lot of trendy folks used to cast a scornful glance over their shoulders as they walked past the plain looking restaurant with all the empty tables in the window. The tables have turned. A lot of discriminating diners now prefer Massimo Natoli's little place where the scale permits acute attention to every morsel that leaves the kitchen. The restaurant has recently undergone an impressive facelift and the trendies have begun to flock in. The veal in champagne sauce is still absolutely perfect.

INDEX

For names in boldface type

Your Suggestions

While using this book, you'll have trekked the wet streets of Vancouver east and west, browsed in bookshops on Pender Street, sampled the sweets of Chinatown and the spicy treats of Commercial Drive; you've gone to a matinee, taken a stadium tour and driven up to Howe Sound.

If it's still raining, write me a note. Tell me about that antique store that looks as if it were flown intact from London's Portobello Road, or that all-night cafe with tap-dancing waiters. With the World's Fair coming up in 1986, there'll be many new places and events. Please share your discoveries with the readers of future editions of this book by writing a letter or postcard to me at P.O. Box 1088, Station A, Vancouver, B.C. V6C 2T1.

By the way, don't let a sudden sunburst get in the way of your rainy-day plan. There isn't a thing in this book that wouldn't adapt to a sudden drying trend. Just toss your umbrella and give thanks to Mother Nature for keeping us guessing.

Paula Brook
Vancouver, Winter 1984

NOTES

NOTES

NOTES

NOTES

NOTES

NOTES

NOTES

NOTES

NOTES

NOTES

NOTES